EASY
JAPANESE

Jack Seward

PASSPORT BOOKS
NTC/Contemporary Publishing Group

This edition first published in 1992 by Passport Books,
a division of NTC/Contemporary Publishing Group, Inc.,
4255 West Touhy Avenue,
Lincolnwood (Chicago), Illinois 60712-1975 U.S.A.
Originally published by Yohan Publications, Inc.
© Yohan Publications, Inc. All rights reserved.
No part of this book may be reproduced, stored
in a retrieval system, or transmitted in any form or by any means,
electronic, mechanical, photocopying, recording or otherwise, without
prior written permission of NTC/Contemporary Publishing Group, Inc.
Manufactured in the United States of America.
International Standard Book Number: 0-8442-8495-5

9 10 11 12 VRS/VRS 0 4 3 2 1

Dedication

For
my stepfather
Jackson L. Newman

TABLE OF CONTENTS

The Author

Jack Seward is a Japan area-and-language specialist whose intimate involvement with Japanese extends over half a century. He has taught college-level courses in Japanese and is the author of many books on the people and country where he lived for 25 years. He and his present wife Aiko Morimoto reside in the State of Texas.

Introduction

Today, as many as 650,000 non-Japanese are said to be trying to learn the Japanese language—a number that should increase to about 4 1/2 million by the century's turn.

Assuming that Japan continues to be the economically successful nation it now is, this worldwide interest in its culture and language may well go on widening even beyond the year 2,000.

EASY JAPANESE has been written in response to the demands of that exploding market and designed for both self-study and classroom instruction.

My own exposure to the speech of then-distant Japan began in 1939 when I learned my first words and accelerated in 1942 with the wartime exigency and my initial formal college course in *Nihongo*. Since then, I have either been living in Japan or studying the language in school or working in a Japanese company in the U.S. (as well as speaking mostly Japanese at home to my Japanese wife). My interest in the language has never waned. In fact, the more I learn, the more I find there is I wish to know.

Thus, the acquisition of linguistic competence has been a lifetime pursuit. Along the way, I have developed ideas of my own about how best to teach this language to beginners who will tread the same path that I trod myself.

Each of the sixteen lessons herein begins with a section on Useful Everyday Expressions, which the student can put to immediate use. (As much as possible, I have tried to avoid the often rather inane examples found elsewhere: "My book is big," "Kiyoko has a cat," and so forth.)

This section is followed by the lesson's vocabulary, many of which items are used in the example sentences in the same lesson.

Almost all of these words are taken from lists of those most frequently used in the language. The English equivalents may be only one word (seldom more than three), and the student should remember that many words may mean more than what a one- or two-word translation says they mean. The student should, therefore, arm himself with dictionaries and develop the habit of referring to them often for fuller explanations.

Thereafter come the Pattern Sentences and then the How to Use section which explains the grammatical forms introduced in that lesson. Next, you will find paragraphs that comment on the cultural milieu in which some of the lesson's expressions are heard, followed by specific Study Recommendations.

Instead of introducing the student to *kana* and *kanji* from the beginning, I have waited till the middle of the text—to give him or her a chance to achieve a certain level of effective verbal communication before buckling down to the rigors of the written language.

Standard (spoken) Japanese is based on the speech of educated persons living in and around Tokyo. Except where otherwise indicated, it is the language presented in this text. Due to advances in public communications, Standard Japanese is understood throughout Japan, although dialectal pockets continue to exist here and there.

The Japanese place more value on emotions than logic, and this is reflected in their language. A **broad-stroke** description of the language would be that it is a tongue with musical rather than stress accents and one in which the grammatical functions are expressed by adjunctive words. There is little distinction between its genders and no explicit plurality or singularity in its nouns. It has no articles (a, an, the) or relative pronouns. Its adjectives do not change in form for purposes of comparison and they can be used as predicates in themselves. Cases are pointed out by particles called **postpositions**. The basic stems of verbs often function as nouns. Modifiers come before modified words and objects before verbs. Subjects generally come first with predicates at the end of the sentences (which is why simultaneous interpretation is not feasible).

Add these features to not-so-difficult pronunciation and you find yourself contemplating a language that you think should be relatively easy. That it is not can be attributed to the complexity of the written language, the sometimes illogical organization of its grammar, and the fact that Japanese developed in isolation from most other tongues (except for its ingestion of the Chinese pictograms).

That you are reading this Introduction leads me to hope that you have made a firm commitment to learn to work with the people of Japan in their own language. Through this series of texts, I would like to lead you to genuine competence in Japanese. I can assure you that this ability will be most beneficial in several ways, not the least of which will be the sheer pleasure that comes from living among the Japanese people as an insider—and not as a stranger.

The author

Lesson One

The Importance of Good Pronunciation

If one particular lesson in this book were to be chosen as the most important, it would have to be the first. Lesson One should be studied with extreme care and, as the text will recommend, should be reviewed several times during the course of these lessons.

The importance of these instructions will become more apparent as the student advances in his studies. Even so, he should become as familiar with them as possible in the initial stage of his acquaintance with Japanese.

Surely it would be an exercise in obtuse perversity to spend hundreds, even thousands of hours mastering the grammar, ideographs, and vocabulary of Japanese, only to deface the final product and seriously hamper its utility by disguising it under the ugly paint of mispronunciation.

Yet this is exactly what happens all too often, even though Japanese pronunciation is really not difficult. Certainly it should be easier for foreigners to master than it is for the Japanese to become skilled in English pronunciation. Still, by far the most common fault among Westerners learning to speak Japanese is *mal*pronunciation. (Other Orientals do not seem to have so much difficulty with Japanese pronunciation.)

Hearing this malpronunciation, one wonders if the would-be speakers are even aware that it is necessary to *learn* correct pronunciation, just as it is essential that they memorize vocabulary and pattern sentences.

The advice offered in this lesson can take the student a good distance down the road toward understandable Japanese pronunciation that does not grate on the ears. But reading these specific instructions

4

should be buttressed by listening to the voices of native Japanese speakers. If the student is living in Japan or closely associated with Japanese in his own country, this will be easy to accomplish. If that recourse is not available to him, he should buy cassette tapes of native speech. These tapes should be played frequently, and the student should repeat the pattern sentences and vocabulary after the speaker.

Important to pronunciation is the question of which system of romanization is used. Bear in mind that romanized Japanese *(rōmaji)* is almost like a foreign language to most Japanese. It was devised to help the foreigner learn their language. The two main systems of romanization are the Hepburn system and the Official System *(Kunrei-shiki)*. The Hepburn system (sometimes called the *Hyōjun-shiki)* is easier for the native English speaker as well as being that used in most Japanese-English dictionaries, in English-language periodicals published in Japan, and in this text. The Official System is rapidly falling into disuse.

Before proceeding to specific rules of pronunciation, a few words of paramount advice must be given to the student.

Since most of us know only one language, it is difficult to give up or set aside the speech habits of a lifetime. Yet this is exactly what the student should strive to do if he is to come to grips with Japanese.

To repeat, Japanese is not really hard to pronounce, and the foreign student can quickly learn to reproduce most of its sounds correctly. But how he puts those sounds together, how he strings out those vowels and consonants that form the syllables is another matter.

Here the student comes to his first hurdle, and it may be the highest one he will have to surmount, with the exception of *kanji* memorization. But it can be done. Have no doubt about that. It requires determination. The student, especially the native speaker of English, must wrench himself free of deeply ingrained habits of speech and clear his speech apparatus—even as one clears his palate with bread before tasting a different wine—for a new way of speaking.

English is spoken with an up-and-down, up-and-down inflection. If we could graphically represent English speech, it would look like a roller coaster. This has been called syncopated speech. The speaker jumps along like a kangaroo to an irregular rhythm based on the English system of heavy syllabic stresses.

Even though each consonant and vowel may be voiced correctly or almost correctly, Japanese spoken in this roller coaster manner is not only unpleasant to hear but does not lend itself to ready comprehension. Japanese auditors may greet this manner of speech with a puzzled laugh.

After clearing his linguistic palate, the student should imagine that he has set a musician's metronome in front of him. Tock-tock-tock-tock-tock goes the metronome. Steady, evenly spaced, unchanging sounds. Monotonous, you might say, and so it is. Very monotonous. But that is exactly the way the student should first try to speak Japanese, with each syllable being given equal stress.

To be sure, there are certain variations in what might be called the prominence of Japanese syllables. These are brought about by factors to be discussed herein. In time, the student's ear will pick up these slight musical accents. He will be able to imitate them himself. Even so, except for a few whispered or voiceless vowels, the student should force himself to speak each syllable distinctly and with equal emphasis and length.

When he does so, he may have the momentarily disconcerting feeling that he is talking like a robot programmed to imitate human sounds, without emotions. Yet it is better to sound this way during his early acquaintance with Japanese than to sound largely incomprehensible during all the succeeding years that he continues to speak the language.

What this means in practice: Take the sentence, *Toshi no sei de mōroku suru* (to become senile in old age). Visualize the syllables as they would be written in *kana*: *To-shi no se-i de mo-o-ro-ku su-ru.* Twelve syllables in all. Each should be voiced with equal emphasis. Try it. Once more. Now you are closer to correct Japanese speech. Never mind that you may sound like a machine. As your studies and practice advance, this metronomic beat, while never disappearing entirely, will merge with the slight natural accents of a native speaker and become less noticeable.

Restrain your natural tendency to let your voice go up-and-down, up-and-down while speaking. Resist the temptation to place stress on certain syllables: TO-shi no SE-i de MO-o-ro-KU su-RU or however. Give equal attention to each syllable except the whispered *u* and *i.* (More about these further on.)

Syllables

Japanese is a language composed of 107 syllables, whereas English is one made up of consonants and vowels as well as syllables (more than 3,000). The table below gives the syllables in Japanese.

These syllables are all written in *kana* (if not *rōmaji*), and when foreign words are used in Japanese, these must be written in *kana,* i.e., in these syllables. It is, therefore, difficult to reproduce foreign language sounds in Japanese exactly. Take the English word 'silver,' for instance. You will see from the table below that Japanese has no *si, l, ve,* or final *r* sounds. Thus, silver must be given as *shi-ru-ba,* if the native word (*gin*) is not to be used.

The only consonant that can be written alone is *n,* in the upper righthand corner of the table.

a	ka	ga	sa	za	ta	da	na	ha	ba	pa	ma	ra	wa	n
i	ki	gi	shi	ji	chi	ji	ni	hi	bi	pi	mi	ri	wo	
u	ku	gu	su	zu	tsu	zu	nu	fu	bu	pu	mu	ru		
e	ke	ge	se	ze	te	de	ne	he	be	pe	me	re		
o	ko	go	so	zo	to	do	no	ho	bo	po	mo	ro		
ya	kya	gya	sha	ja	cha	ja	nya	hya	bya	pya	mya	rya		
yu	kyu	gyu	shu	ju	chu	ju	nyu	hyu	byu	pyu	myu	ryu		
yo	kyo	gyo	sho	jo	cho	jo	nyo	hyo	byo	pyo	myo	ryo		

Four other syllables—*fa, fe, fi, fo*—can be written in *kana* but are used only in foreign words or names.

Vowels

The five Japanese vowels have one—and only one—pronunciation each:

> *a*   as in f*a*ther
> *i*   as in macaron*i*
> *u*   as in Z*u*l*u*
> *e*   as in *e*dge or m*e*lody
> *o*   as in s*o*l*o* or *o*asis

A sharp contrast is made between long and short vowels. The long vowel is twice as long as the short vowel. In written Japanese, the long vowel is given the space of two syllables and should be spoken as if it were two syllables. Thus, *ō* is said as *o-o*. Not separately but just longer. The long vowel is shown by a bar overhead, called a macron: i.e, *ā* and *ū*.

Some romanized versions of Japanese will show a vowel's long sound by repeating the vowel and not using the macron: *Chuubei* instead of *Chūbei,* for Central America. Usually, this text will employ the macron.

It is customary, however, to write the long *i* sound as *ii* and not as *ī,* as in *utsukushii,* for beautiful, and *chiisai* for small. Also, in verb endings, it is better to repeat a vowel than draw a bar over it: *kuu* instead of *kū,* to eat; *nuu* instead of *nū,* to sew.

The student will make many laughable, if not disastrous mistakes if he does not pay close heed to the distinction between short and long vowels. *Omachigai* is an honorable (meaning your) mistake; *ōmachigai* is a great mistake. *Tori* is a bird; *tōri* is a street. *Komon* is an advisor; *kōmon* is the anal exit. *Shoten* is a book shop; *shōten* is any store. The list goes on, ad infinitum.

A Japanese vowel can follow any other vowel or can follow itself. In English, two vowels in succession form a diphtong, i.e., 'ae,' and are spoken as one syllable. In Japanese, however, each such vowel must be given the sound value of a separate syllable: *a,* then *e.*

Outside Japan, the benighted will reproduce Japanese place

names, personal names, and even words without the macron's benefit. Added to the usual way in which Japanese is mangled away from Japan, this leads to utter incomprehension and even to the creation of international incidents. If, in London, we talk about "Mr. Oe," our Japanese listener has no idea if we mean Mr. Oe (小江さん) or Mr. Ōe (大江さん), since we make no distinction.

Another frequent mistake made abroad (and even in Japan) is to pronounce the vowel *o* as if it were *a*. Thus, the Honda motor car becomes the "Handa" (*handa* means solder).

The Whispered Vowels

In Japanese, the vowels *i* and *u* are often devoiced or whispered. Sometimes they seem almost lost between any pair of the following consonants or consonant combinations: *ch, f, h, k, p, s, sh, ts,* and *t*. Pronounce them as shown in these examples: *kusa* (grass) as if it were *k'sa, shita* (tongue or under) as if it were *sh'ta, kita* (north) as if it were *k'ta,* and *shichi* (seven) as if it were *sh'chi*.

The devoiced final *u* is particularly noticeable in *desu* (the polite verb for am, are, is) and in the respectful verb-ending *-masu*. (The major exception is in dialectal speech, notably that of the women of Kyoto.) This devocalization is indicated in romanized Japanese, if at all, by a line under the *u* (*desu̲*), omission of the *u* (*des*), slashing of the *u* (*desu̸*), replacement of the *u* with an apostrophe (*des'*), enclosing it in parenthesis *des(u)*, or by a small curve above the *u* (*desŭ*). This text, however, prefers to rely on the student's memory, with occasional textual reminders.

With the muted or whispered final *u, desu* and *-masu* become almost like *dess* and *-mass*.

Consonants

The consonants *b, d, j, k, m, n, p,* and *t* are voiced as in English.

Before a vowel, *s* is pronounced as in *s*almon.

Sh is said as in *sh*arp.

Ch is voiced as in *ch*eat.

Other consonants are sounded as noted below.

Consonants prefixed to syllables beginning with *y*, e.g. *kya, kyo, kyu, rya, ryo, ryu, mya, myu, myo, hya, hyo, hyu, nya, nyo,* and *nyu* may give momentary pause to the beginner. He should, however, be able to master them quickly. Let the sound of the initial consonant blend in with that of the following syllable. Since, with the single exception of *n*, there are no consonants that can be written alone in the *kana* syllabary, the initial consonants in the sounds given above cannot be written as *k, r, m, h,* or *n*, but must be written as *ki, ri, mi, hi,* or *ni*.

In *kana*, the succeeding syllable is often written smaller and below and slightly to the right of the preceding symbol, instead of directly below, to indicate that the two sounds should be blended rather than given two completely separate sound values. Thus, きゅ, りょ, and みゃ for *kyu, ryo,* and *mya*.

Double Consonants

Double consonants are frequent in Japanese—and are frequently mispronounced. The root of the trouble appears to be failure to treat the consonants as separate syllables.

For instance, take the word *otte* (pursuer). The beginner is tempted to pronounce this word as if it contained only two syllables, i.e., *o* and *te*. What then comes forth sounds more like "your hand" or "honorable hand" *(o-te)* than "pursuer" *(otte)*. When you learn the *kana* syllabary, however, you can see that *otte* is written with the three *kana* symbols お *(o)*, つ *(tsu)*, and て *(te)*, which may make it easier to remember to treat the additional consonant as a separate syllable.

Done correctly, there is a slight pause after the first *t* (written *tsu*) in *otte*, after which the final syllable *te* is released in a small explosion of breath. Some texts show this pause with an apostrophe, as in *shin'nen* (New Year). This same breath explosion can also be heard in pronouncing the double consonants *kk,* as in *makka* (bright red), and *pp,* as in *shuppan* (publishing).

Similar care should be taken with all the double consonants in Japanese, as in these words: *bummei* (civilization), *suppai* (sour), *kakke* (beri-beri), *kekkon* (marriage), *zatto* (roughly), *sonnō* (reverence for the emperor), and *kissaten* (coffee shop).

The puff of breath, called an aspiration, that accompanies such double or triple consonants as *kk, tt, pp, ss, tch,* and *ssh* is preceded by a slight tensing of the throat muscles.

The Consonant g

The initial *g* in Japanese is hard, as in goal, with the exception of the postposition *ga,* where it is soft. Here are some examples: *gorotsuki* (ruffian), *gesubatta koto wo iu* (to talk vulgarly), and *gumpō-kaigi* (court-martial).

Within a word, *g* is softer, as in *eiga* (movie), *kagaku* (science or chemistry), *mago* (grandchild), and *fushigi* (strange, wonderful, unaccountable).

H

An *h* before *i* or *y* is something like sh in the English "ship" and *ch* in the German *ich.* Examples for practice are: *hidoi* (harsh, severe, unfair), *hijō ni* (extremely), *hin* (quality), *hi no kuruma* (extreme poverty), *hyō* (leopard), and *hyōmen* (surface, exterior).

n

N is the only consonant in Japanese to stand alone. As a single consonant, it comes only at the end of a syllable (except when it is used as an abbreviation for *no*), and should be accorded special attention. It has a nasal sound and should be given the force of a single syllable.

The unwary student might be tempted to pronounce *San-in* (that part of southwestern Honshu facing the Japan Sea) as if it were two syllables, i.e., *San* and *in*. It is, instead, four—and this is easier to understand when one sees that *San-in* is written in *kana* with four symbols (さんいん), each of which should be pronounced as a separate syllable.

Before *b, m,* and *p,* this *n* is pronounced as *m.* The 1954 edition of *Kenkyusha's New Japanese-English Dictionary* retains the *n* spelling, as in *shinbun* (newspaper), whereas the 1949 edition gives *shimbun.* In this text, I have chosen to follow the phonetic rendering: *amma* (massage), *jimbutsu* (person, character), *sampatsu* (haircutting), and, of course, *shimbun.*

This *n* before *ch, d, j, t, ts,* or another *n* is pronounced with the tip of the tongue behind the upper teeth. Remember to elongate it and to give it the value of a full syllable in words like these: *kichinto* (exactly), *banji* (all things), *hannichi kanjō* (anti-Japanese feeling), and *shinchiku* (new building).

Before *k* or *g,* this *n* is pronounced as if it were *ng,* as in: *anki* (memorization), *hanketsu* (verdict or decree), *benki* (bedpan), *ringetsu* (the last month of pregnancy), and *kankaku* (sensation, feeling). In these examples, pronounce *hanketsu* like *ha-ng-ke-tsu, benki* like *be-ng-ki, ringetsu* like *ri-ng-ge-tsu,* and *kankaku* like *ka-ng-ka-ku.*

When it precedes *y* or *w* or any vowel, this *n* borrows a bit of the sound which follows, as in: *bun'ya*(field or specialty), *danwa* (talk, colloquy), and *shin-ō* (epicenter). Note that when *n* precedes the vowels *i* or *e,* a *y* sound (as in young) is slightly voiced, as in *shin-ei* (pro-British), which is pronounced *shin-(y) ei,* or *sen-i* (textile, fiber), which is pronounced *sen-(y)i.* When the *n* comes before *y,* as in *gyūnyū* (milk), it is pronounced like the Spanish *n* in *señor,* with the middle part of the tongue touching the roof of the mouth and the breath passing partly through the mouth and partly through the nose.

When the *n* is at the end of a word, it is pronounced (still with the value of a full syllable) with the tongue near but not quite touching the roof of the mouth. Examples are: *ampan* (a sweet, jam-filled bun), *bin* (bottle), and *jitaku bumben* (child delivery at home). This same pronunciation applies when *n* precedes *f, h, r, s, sh,* and *z*, as in these examples: *tansan* (carbonic acid, a brand of carbonated water), *shinsha* (new car), *manzai* (a comic stage dialogue), *shinrō* (bridegroom), *Taiwan-fū* (Taiwan style), and *shinri* (mentality).

Tsu

Tsu may seem to rank after *r* in difficulty with most foreign students, but the correct way of saying it can be readily taught.

Extend the tip of the tongue just through the nearly closed teeth and try to say the girl's name Sue. Think of it as the ts in its. But don't forget the *u*.

There you have it.

The Tapped R

The *r* in Japanese distinguishes the speech of most foreigners, particularly Americans, from true Japanese more clearly than any other aspect of pronunciation. Foreign speakers have difficulty with this *r*, even as the Japanese have trouble with the *l* sound in English. It would be fair to say that just as the *l* sound does not exist in Japanese, the Japanese *r* does not exist in English—or in numerous other foreign tongues.

Yet, the *r* sound is really not that hard. A modicum of concentration, a dash of careful mimicry, and a soupcon of memory can take the student over this barrier with little need for dismay.

A blending of the d, r, and l of English, this *r* is made by letting the tongue tap the gum ridge just above and behind the upper teeth. It then descends.

Try saying the English name Eddy, pronouncing the dd very

briefly. This should produce a close approximation of the Japanese word for collar: *eri.*

Practice the *r* by repeating, *Rikutsuppoi hōrōsha no rireki* (an argumentative tramp's personal history) and progress to *Ruri-chan no rippa na rappa wa uraremashita ka.* (Has Ruri's fine bugle been sold?).

The F in Japanese

In English, the *f* is made by placing the lower lip against the upper teeth. (For instance, the hard *'f'* in flip.)

The Japanese *f,* however, is lighter than the *f* in English. The Japanese don't use the teeth at all. They bring the lips almost together, as if about to whistle, and then blow the *f* out with a very slight puff. Practice this *f* with words like these: *fude* (writing brush), *fuyu* (winter), *futoru* (to be fat, big), *fūtō* (envelope), and *futsuka-yoi* (hangover, lit., second-day drunkenness.)

Remember the Japanese *f* as a light English *f* without any teeth in it.

Wa and Wo in Japanese

When *wo,* the postposition indicating the accusative case, follows a word ending in *n,* it is pronounced with the lips stretched slightly outward—as in the beginning of a smile—and not rounded. For example: *Sono jigyō ni hyakuman wo tōshi shita* (I invested a million in that enterprise).

When, however, it comes after a word ending in a vowel, e.g., *hiyō wo motsu* (to bear expenses), the *w* is nearly inaudible. It is so nearly inaudible, in fact, that some textbooks give *o* instead of *wo* for this postposition. It is, however, written with the *kana* symbol for *wo* （を） instead of that for *o* （お）.

When saying *wa* (usually following the subject of a sentence) in Japanese, you should relax your lips, leaving them a little slack. The lips are not rounded so *wa* sounds at times almost like *a.*

Accent and Pitch

Accent in Japanese is a matter of higher or lower musical pitch, of which there are three degrees—low, mid, and high. Where the pitch will fall is entirely unpredictable, and so rules—even general ones—are impossible. To worsen matters, in Kansai and in parts of Kyushu and Shikoku the pitch is the opposite of what we hear in the standard Japanese (*hyōjungo*) spoken in and around Tokyo.

What saves the day, however, is that the degree of variance in pitch is so small that the beginner is advised to voice all Japanese words, with the exceptions of the devocalized *i* and *u* noted above, with a steady evenness of pitch. You should, in fact, extend this monotony of pitch to entire sentences, taking care to use little if any of the rising interrogative inflection of English in the spoken Japanese question mark *ka*. Sooner or later, depending on the sharpness of your ear, you will come to be able to distinguish among and mimic the existing minor variations in pitch, and, in the meantime, almost nothing will have been lost. Pitch will be the least of your problems in learning Japanese.

Someone may point out to you the three *hashi* (bridge, chopsticks, and edge) and caution that you cannot distinguish among the three without proper pitch. Pay him no heed. No one is going to rush at you on a dark night shouting *"Hashi!"* and then run on, leaving you to wonder if you should reach for your trusty *chopsticks,* sharpen the *edge* of your samurai sword, or sprint for the *bridge* before the creek rises.

Context will save the day—or the night. The Japanese guest in your dining room who asks for *hashi* will have little use for edges and none for bridges.

Summary

To ask the student to digest all the above in one sitting would be unreasonable.

Instead, he should go through it carefully, retaining as much as his memory permits. Later, he should review this lesson often. (The text will remind him to do so.)

For the present, however, at least remember the following as you proceed into the succeeding lessons:

1. How to pronounce the five vowels.
2. Treat the double consonants as *two* syllables.
3. Tap out the *r*. (Flick the tip of the tongue against the gum ridge above the inner teeth.)
4. *Tsu* starts out like the ts in its.
5. Flex your lips before speaking Japanese. Exaggerated mobility is not required, but at least get more lip motion into your speech than some stiff-lipped persons do.
6. Speak like a metronome, not like a roller coaster.

Lesson Two

A.) Word Order
B.) Particles *Wa, Ga, Mo, Ka, Ne,* and *Yo*
C.) Singulars and Plurals
D.) *Desu* and *Arimasu*
E.) Yes and No.

Useful Everyday Expressions

Konnichi wa	Used after mid-morning, this phrase means hello, good day, or good afternoon. This and the *komban wa* that follows are used to outsiders and not to classmates, family members, or coworkers, because they sound formal and distant. Further, they should not be said to superiors.
Komban wa	Good evening. (Note comments above).
Ohayō (gozaimasu)	Used until about ten a.m., this means good morning and can be said to anyone. *Ohayō* is plain or familiar; *ohayō gozaimasu* is the standard polite expression and the one you should use mostly.
Jā, ato de	See you later.
Sayōnara (or *Sayonara*)	Goodbye. This word is used when the parting is likely to be for an extended period. When leaving your office at the end of the day, you would not say *sayōnara,* unless you have just quit your job or perhaps are leaving on a round-the-world sales trip. Also, the Japanese avoid using the word to a superior, because it does not sound polite. Do not use it to a member of your family, unless you do not expect to see him again.

Vocabulary

sensei	teacher	*tsukue*	desk
isu	chair	*uma*	horse
jisho	dictionary	*bengoshi*	lawyer

*otoko**	man	*kakimasu*	I, you, they write,
*onna***	woman		he or she writes
kodomo	child		(the *-masu* ending
empitsu	pencil		is the polite form in
bunkei	pattern sentence		the present and fu-
kanji	ideograph, written		ture tenses)
	character	*iimasu*	(1) say (see above)
neko	cat	*aimasu*	(I) meet
hon	book	*ikimasu*	(I) go
eiga	movie	*tabemasen*	(I) do not eat.
kana	the *hiragana* or		(negative of *tabema-*
	katakana syllabary		*su* or I do eat, will
	symbols		eat.)
seito	student, pupil	*mimasen*	(I) do not see
isha	medical doctor		(negative of *mima-*
Kanada	Canada		*su* or I see)
Amerika	America	*sakana*	fish
Kankoku	Korea	*hannin*	criminal
Nihon	Japan	*seijika*	politician
Taiwan	Taiwan	*watakushi*	I
Chūgoku	China	*boku*	I (used mostly by
Indoneshia	Indonesia		boys & young men)
Marēshia	Malaysia	*-jin*	person. Not used
Doitsu	Germany		alone. Added to
hai	yes (I'm listening)		name of a country.
ē	yes		Thus, *Nihon-jin* for
Wa-ei	Japanese-English		Japanese, *Tai-jin*
	(from *kanji* for		for Thai, etc.
	Japan and England)	*kirei*	pretty, neat, nice
*anata****	you (polite)	*ato (de)*	later
takusan	many, much	*atsui*	thick (can also
kyō	today		mean hot, if written
iie	no (pronounced as		with a different
	i-i-(y)e)		*kanji*)
minikui	ugly	*kibishii*	strict, hard, severe,
yobisute	calling a person's		stern
	family name with-	*sono*	that (adjectival
	out adding a polite		pronoun)
	suffix	*doko*	where
hachiji	eight o'clock	*nani, nan*	what
	(*hachi* is eight and	*dare*	who
	ji means the hour)	*gaijin*	foreigner
		mampuku	full stomach

kekkō	fine, good, excellent	*no shita ni*	under, beneath
itsu	when	*no ue ni*	over, above
koko	here	*hima*	free time
soko	there		

* *otoko no hito* means the same as *otoko* but is politer.

** *onna no hito* means the same as *onna* but is politer.

*** As soon as he learns the word *anata,* the foreign student is tempted to use it whenever he would use 'you' in English. It is not, however, used nearly so often. Other pronouns or even proper names and titles may be used instead, as we will see later, or certain polite forms of verbs may indicate about whom we are talking without recourse to *anata.*

This is not to say that *anata* is not heard at all. It is used among women of the same age group and status. A mother may call her child *anata* but not vice versa. A teacher may address his pupil as *anata* but would be upset if the pupil used the same pronoun to him in return.

In the early stages of your studies, however, you may find it hard not to use a pronoun meaning 'you.' If so, you may be forced to use *anata,* but remember that one day you will learn better ways to express the same idea. Further, while cautioning against it, this text may use it occasionally in the pattern sentences, at least until the 'better ways' have been introduced.

Pattern Sentences

(Bunkei)

Note: The pattern sentence method of language instruction approximates the natural way a child learns language—by imitating the speech of adults around it. The structure of these pattern sentences, called *bunkei* in Japanese, should be repeated over and over by the student. As he increases his vocabulary, he can make appropriate substitutions in the memorized pattern sentence structure. Pattern Sentence No. One below, for example, can thereby be expanded to:

Sensei wa Doitsu-jin desu.	The teacher is a German.
Seito wa Marēshia-jin desu.	The student is a Malaysian.
Isha wa hannin desu.	The doctor is a criminal.
	(Or, Doctors are criminals.)
Sono otoko wa seijika desu.	That man is a politician.

Sono kodomo wa Indoneshia-   The child is an Indonesian.
jin desu.

(And so forth, ad infinitum)

Another reason for the importance of memorizing the pattern sentences is that they are natural or native Japanese. Many foreigners learn vocabulary and some grammatical guidelines, then put together their own sentences. They may be understood, and no Japanese would ever correct them, but these foreigners do not speak the way a native Japanese would.

In any event, implant the pattern sentences in your memories.

1. *Sensei wa Taiwan-jin desu.*   The teacher is a Taiwanese.

2. *Kibishii sensei wa hima ga arimasu.* The difficult (strict) teacher has free time.

3. *Chūgoku-jin no sensei wa kanji wo kirei ni kakimasu.*
   The Chinese teacher writes ideographs neatly.

4. *Isu ni nani ga arimasu ka.   Wa-ei jiten ga arimasu.*
   What is on the chair?   A Japanese-English dictionary is (on the chair).

5. *Anata wa Nihon-jin desu ka.   Hai, Nihon-jin desu.*
   Are you a Japanese?   Yes, (I) am a Japanese.

6. *Watakushi mo Amerika-jin desu.*   I too am an American.

7. *Takusan no hon ga tsukue no ue ni arimasu.*
   Many books are on top of the desk.

8. *Sono minikui onna no hito wa Kankoku-jin ja arimasen.*
   That ugly woman is not Korean.

9. *Empitsu wa doko desu ka.   Empitsu wa doko ni arimasu ka.*
   Both mean, Where is the (a) pencil?

10. *Koko ni mo soko ni mo arimasu.*   (Pencils) are both here and there.

11. *Kimura-san wa ikimasu ka.   Iie, watakushi ga ikimasu.*
    Is Mr. Kimura going?   No, *I* will go.

12. *Kyō wa samui yo.*   It is cold today. (Today is cold.)

13. *Anata ka watakushi ka ga ikimasu.*   Either you or I will go.

14. *Boku wa iimasu yo.*   I will say it.   *Boku ga iimasu yo.*
    I will say it.

15. *Eiga wa mimasen ka?* Aren't you going to watch the (a) movie?
16. *Sono neko wa sakana mo tabemasen.* That cat does not even eat fish.
17. *Ē, sō desu.* Yes, it is so.
18. *Hashimura to iimasu ga Doi-san wa imasu ka?* My name is Hashimura; Is Mr. (Mrs., Miss) Doi in?
19. *Watakushi wa Doi desu ga....* I am Doi, (but)... (Is there something I can do for you?)
20. *Boku wa Indo-jin desu.* I am an Indian. *Boku ga Indo-jin desu.* I am the Indian.
21. *Sono gaijin wa hen desu.* That foreigner is odd. (Sometimes used to mean, That foreigner can speak Japanese. Until recent years, foreigners who could speak competent Japanese were so rare as to be considered oddities or even spies).

How to Use
Word Order

The usual word order in Japanese is:

Subject—object—verb	See *Bunkei* No. 3
Subject—adjective	See *Bunkei* No. 12
Remote subject—immediate subject—verb	See *Bunkei* No. 2

The last word order above (Remote subject—immediate subject—verb) requires explanation. The Japanese often begin a sentence with a noun, pronoun, or substantive that can be called the 'topic' or 'remote' or 'notional' subject. With this word, they set the stage for what they are about to say. In effect, what they are saying is, "Now, this is what I am going to talk about." In *Bunkei* No. 12 the speaker says, "Now, I am going to talk about 'today' *(kyō)*: Well, it is cold." The *wa* that follows it can be given as 'as for' or 'as concerns.' Thus, "Today—as for—Well, it is cold."

Often, there is no subject at all, it being understood, as in the second part of *Bunkei* No. 5.

You should, as you progress, try to see how often you can indicate the subjects of your sentences through such alternative means as the plain and polite forms of verbs.

There is some flexibility in word order. For instance, we may say *Watakushi wa kanojo ni aimashita* (I met her) or *Kanojo ni watakushi wa aimashita* (I met her). What is not flexible, however, is the position of the main predicate (verb) at the end of the sentence.

Particles

Wa and *ga* usually follow the subjects (remote or immediate) of sentences. Much has been said about the difficulty in understanding the difference between *wa* and *ga,* but it should not be hard. Note that emphasis is one difference: *ga* is more emphatic than *wa.* In the second part of *Bunkei* No. 11 above, *watakushi* or I is emphasized; thus, it is followed by *ga.* Also, there is the difference between the *wa* used after the remote subject and the *ga* used after the immediate subject, as explained above. See *Bunkei* No. 2.

Still another difference is that *ga* is always used after question words, such as *nani* or *nan* (what), *dare* (who), *itsu* (when), and so forth. See *Bunkei* No. 4.

It is customary to use *ga* after the immediate subject when the predicate that follows is a form of *aru* (to be, have), *iru* (to need), *dekiru* (to be able to do), and *hoshii* (to be desired):

O-sake ga arimasu.	I have sake.
O-sake ga irimasu.	I need sake.
O-sake wo kau koto ga dekimasen.	I cannot buy sake.
O-sake ga hoshii desu.	I want sake.

At times *wa*—but not *ga*—is substituted for the accusative marker *wo* for emphasis or contrast. (See *Bunkei* No. 15.) This is somewhat more common in negative sentences but can also be heard in affirmative ones as well.

Tabako wa suimasen ga o-sake wa nomimasu.
I don't smoke cigarettes, but I drink sake.

Whereas the English 'but' is used to introduce a contrary statement, the Japanese *ga* at times is more similar to 'and' in meaning, although it still may be translated as 'but'. See *Bunkei* No. 18.

In a like manner, *ga* can also be added to a word or sentence to invite the listener's reply, as in *Bunkei* No. 19. It is also used to soften the force of a positive declarative sentence. (See Cultural Sidelights below.)

While keeping these comments in mind, the student should—for the present—rely largely on the near-memorization of pattern sentences in which *wa* and *ga* are used. These will implant natural usage in his mind.

Mo means 'also' and can be used in place of *wa, ga,* and *wo.* See *Bunkei* Nos. 6 and 10. It may also mean 'even', as in *Bunkei* No. 16.

Another way of thinking of the particles *wa, ga, wo, ni,* and *no* is as 'case markers.' More precisely, *wa* may be called the topic marker, *ga* the subject marker, *wo* the accusative marker, *ni* the indirect object or dative marker, and *no* the possessive or genitive marker. Note the use of all in the following sentence: *Wagasha wa chingin ga yasui kara minna no kodomo ni michibata de hana-uri wo itsumo sasete imasu.* Because the wages at our company are so low, we always have all our children out selling flowers on the streets.

Ka is the spoken question mark. When it is used at the end of an interrogative sentence, the voice may be raised slightly but without as much elevation as is usually given to the last word in a question in English. In speech, the *ka* is sometimes omitted, particularly by women. When omitted, the last word in the question tends to be elevated a little. When the *ka* is omitted in the written language. the English question mark is used to indicate the interrogative nature of the preceding words, since voice elevation cannot be relied on in writing. See *Bunkei* No. 4, 5, 9, and 11.

This will be discussed later, but *ka* can also have the meaning of 'or', as in *Bunkei* No. 13.

Whereas *ka* is a spoken question mark, *yo* should be thought of as a spoken exclamation mark (!). It is used to add force to what one has said. See *Bunkei* No. 14.

Singulars and Plurals

Japanese nouns have no plural forms. That is, the word *bengoshi* can mean either lawyer or lawyers. Context will usually tell you which. In case plurality or singularity must be shown more clearly, there are ways to do so, i.e. *Kanada-jin* for one Canadian and *Kanada-jin-tachi* for several Canadians or *uma* for a horse and *santō no uma* for three (head of) horses. Generally, however, this is not common. More about this in the relevant lesson.

Throughout this text, the student should keep in mind the possibility of a plural state as well as a singular whenever he finds a noun.

Desu and Arimasu

Doubtless, *desu* and *arimasu* are the two most useful verbs in Japanese. Strictly speaking, they are copulas and like the English 'to be.' It requires, however, three verbs in Japanese (add *imasu* to these two) to do the work usually done by forms of 'to be' in English. (Remember that the *u* in all three is whispered.)

Both *desu* and *arimasu* are polite forms, as is *imasu*. As you will learn, the Japanese speak and write in several levels of politeness. Broadly, these levels can be divided into two classifications that have been variously called the polite and plain, formal and informal, courteous and rough, and respectful and familiar. This text prefers the first: the polite and the plain.

Desu means is, am, or are, as given below:

Present tense	*desu (da)*	is, am, are (lacking another subject, 'there' is understood)

Past tense	*deshita (datta)*	was, were
Future		
conjectural	*deshō (darō)*	may be
Conditional	*deshitara (dattara)*	if there is, if there are

Da is the plain equivalent of *desu*. The other plain equivalents are given in parentheses above.

Do not be confused if you hear a Japanese say to a waiter, *Watakushi wa unagi desu*. Knowing that *desu* means 'am,' you may wonder if the man is saying, "I am an eel." Actually, however, he is saying, "I will have the eel." Literally, I—as for—it is the eel (that I want).

Whereas *desu* makes a connection between the subject noun and another noun, or adjective, *arimasu* states the existence of something. See *Bunkei* Nos. 2, 4, 7, and 9. It can also mean to have, hold, as in *Bunkei* No. 2.

Present tense	*arimasu (aru)*	(there) exist(s), I have, (he, she) has
Past tense	*arimashita (atta)*	(there) existed, I had
Future		
conjectural	*arimashō (arō)*	(there) may exist, I may have
Conditional	*arimashitara (attara or areba)*	if there is, if there are, if (she, he) has
Gerund	*arimashite (atte)*	being, having
Probable past	*arimashita deshō (attarō)*	there probably was
Past Conditional	*arimashita to sureba (atta to sureba)*	if there was, if there were, if (he, she) had
	arimashita nara(ba), [atta nara(ba)]	if there was, if there were, if (he, she) had

Aru is the plain equivalent of *arimasu*. Until the student becomes familiar with patterns of correct social conduct and speech among the Japanese, he is urged not to experiment too freely with the 'plain' forms of communication. To be sure, he must practice these words in order to lodge them in his memory. But take care. Important relationships can be damaged by speaking too "plainly". This advice should be heeded especially by native speakers of English, who, by and large, use the same words to one and all. In Japan, this would be risky.

Aru is usually thought of as the 'to be' verb for inanimate objects while *iru* serves as 'to be' for animate objects. There is one situation, however, where *aru* is used with animate objects, and that is when you speak of relatives and positions. For instance, *Uchi wa hitori no musume to futari no musuko ga arimasu.* (We have one daughter and two sons.) Also, *Amerika wa ō-sama ga arimasen.* (In America, there is no king.) In some situations, either verb can be used: *Neya ni uma ga arimasu (imasu) ka.* Is there a horse (or horses) in the barn?

Aru can be converted to the equivalent of *desu* by introducing *de* before it:

de arimasu = *desu*
de arimashō = *deshō*
de arimashita = *deshita*
de atte = *de*
(and so forth)

De arimasu is somewhat more formal than *desu* and is used more in the written language.

There is another level of politeness above *desu* and *arimasu:* specifically, *de gozaimasu* and *gozaimasu.* For the present, let us set these aside, while using the plain *da* and *aru* with caution.

Yes and No

Both *hai* and *ē* can mean *yes.* For this meaning, the latter is used more often than the former. While meaning yes, *hai* is also used to convey, "I am listening." "Go ahead with what you are saying." But it does not necessarily signify agreement or acquiescence.

Iie means 'no,' but it is not used alone as often as 'no' is used in English. It seems to sound too strong, too emphatic for Japanese tastes. Its promiscuous use, except when a negative answer to a question of fact ("Is this a ¥100 coin?") is required or when one denies praise of himself, can even harm a relationship. The Japanese often prefer to use the negative form of the verb, without a 'no' *(iie)* preceding it.

Sometimes *iie* is said more like *iya* or is repeated quickly: *ie-ie.*

Asked the question, Will you eat this? the English-speaker may reply No or No, I won't. If a Japanese is asked the same question, *Tabemasen ka,* he *could* answer *Iie* (No) or even *Iie, tabemasen* (No, I won't eat it) and be perfectly understood. His preference, however, would be to answer *Tabemasen* (I won't eat it), thereby avoiding *iie* entirely. To be sure, it is even more likely that he would say something like *Kekkō desu* (It's fine), meaning he is fine without eating anything or, *Mampuku desu,* meaning his stomach is full.

In positive utterances, *hai* and *iie* are used in the same sense as in English, but in the case of negative questions, their role may be reversed.

When asked *Tabemasen ka?* (Won't you eat this?), a Japanese may answer, *Hai, tabemasen,* (Yes, I won't eat it). This has given risen to confusion, to put the matter mildly. It is, therefore, just as well that we think of *Hai* as meaning, That's right, and *Iie* as meaning, That's wrong.

When we do, *Hai, tabemasen* becomes, That's right. I won't eat it.

Faced with the same question, had a Japanese wanted to say that he *would* eat it, he might have answered, *Iie, tabemasu* (No, I will eat it.) But again, if we think of *Iie* as being That's wrong, then his reply changes to That's wrong. I *will* eat it.

Another favored way of expressing the negative without using *iie* is to say, *Chigaimasu. Chigau* is the dictionary form of this verb, meaning to be different. Adding *-masu* to its stem *(chigai-)* makes it polite. This word can be translated as No, It is not so, or It is different. Thus, *Anata wa Amerika no daitōryō desu ka* (Are you the president of America?) can be answered with *Chigaimasu* (No, I am not)—unless, of course, you really are the president.

One situation in which the Japanese can be quite emphatic in their use of *iie* is when they deny that anything about themselves or those close to them is superior or even tolerably good. They have found that the more they humble themselves, the more they strengthen the relationship with their listener. Or, in reverse, if their listener is playing the humble role, then they must insist on his good qualities in clear, ringing tones.

Obviously, you can carry this too far, especially among close friends. If, for instance, you are a world-class equestrian, you would not want to say that you have fallen off every horse you ever got on. Remember that "too humble is half-proud."

Cultural sidelights:

A scholar once wrote that he could readily understand the culture of any country by learning the language but that he would hesitate to try to do so without genuine ability in its language. Here, we will try to enhance this process by offering specific explanations of the cultural facets of the Japanese people as they appear in the words and phrases you are learning.

*** Added to the end of a name, *-san* means Mr., Mrs., or Miss. The Japanese do not use *-san* about themselves or about anyone close to them when speaking to outsiders. It almost always should be suffixed to the names of others, however, except as noted below. Failure to do so is called *yobisute* and is very rude, indeed. Depending on age, sex, and how long you have known the other person, there are several exceptions. For the present, however, call your Japanese friends by their family name plus *-san,* (It can be added to both the family and the given names.)
The use of *-san,* however, implies not only respect but also a fairly intimate relationship. For instance, famous statesmen and scholars are often mentioned without the addition of *-san* to their names. To add *-san* would suggest you know them personally. Also, in periodicals, *-san* is normally suffixed to the names of ordinary people until they are charged with a crime. Then it is dropped.

*** Japanese is what is called a confirmation language, meaning that both parties to a dialog should frequently say *hai* or *ē* or make sounds like *hā* or *un* or ask *Sō desu ka* (Is that so?) during brief pauses in the speech of their vis-a-vis. It lets the other party know you are listening attentively and participating actively in the talk. This is called *aizuchi* (lit., two blacksmiths striking an anvil alternately) or response words.

On television, we often see an authority on something or other being interviewed by an attractive young woman called an *aizuchi bijin* or *aizuchi* beauty. Her function is to prompt the authority with appropriate questions, flatter him, and urge him on with sounds of wonderment, admiration, and curiosity. If in English, her comments would be such as, You don't say! How marvellous! That's incredible! Please tell me more. How you must have suffered! Is that so? I'm amazed.

Anyway, do not—repeat, do not—make the mistake of assuming that *hai* or *ē* always means yes. This can lead to emotional turmoil or financial ruin.

*** To the Japanese, vagueness is a virtue. (But it is the speakers who are vague, not the language itself.) Being positive or precise may be regarded as a form of impertinence. Making a positive, precise statement like "I will meet you at eight o' clock" may leave the impression that the listener is not being given a choice. Therefore, the Japanese prefer to say, *Hachiji ni aimasu ga...* or I will meet you at eight o'clock (but)... By adding *ga,* the speaker tells his listener that he is willing to consider other times for the meeting. A similar usage is when, for example, you ask at another's door if Mr. Hashimoto is at home. An affirmative answer might be *Hai, imasu ga...* [Yes, he is here (but)...] Hearing this, you may take alarm, suspecting that the unspoken half of the sentence will be something like "... but he is dying." Actually, however, what can be inferred is, "Shall I summon him?" or possibly, "Who is calling?" Then, when the person you want to see comes forth, he may well say, *Hashimoto desu ga ...* [I am Hashimoto (but)...] This really means, I am Hashimoto. How can I help you?

*** Whereas we in the West tend to regard human beings as the center of the universe, the Japanese attach more importance to the natural world. Further, their natural reticence and modesty drive them to say less about themselves and more about the other person, so the pronoun subject of a sentence is not used as often in Japanese as in English and other languages. Frequent use of 'I' and 'me' sounds assertive and egotistical. (See *Bunkei* Nos. 5 and 18). Often the subject of a sentence can be indicated by polite verbs and verb endings, so about 60% of Japanese sentences manage without subjects. Even if invisible, foreigners with excellent pronunciation in Japanese can often be distinguished from native speakers by their over-usage of *watakushi* (I or me). Although for a different reason, the personal pronouns for you, he, she, and they are not heard as often as in English, either.

*** The Japanese extend their profound respect for education to all teachers. The word *sensei* (literally, first-born) is widely used in addressing teachers of all ranks and categories. Sometimes, it is used about persons with no relation to the formal education process but who have wide experience in certain fields and who can conceivably impart information about it. For instance, the author once knew a thirty-year-old semi-literate fashion model of considerable experience who was often called *sensei* by younger models and other *tori-maki* (hangers-on) in the fashion business. All medical doctors are addressed as *sensei*.

The word can also mean, with jovial disrespect, 'fellow.'

Study recommendations:

The student should carry and use vocabulary cards with the English word or sentence on one side and the Japanese equivalent on the other. He should be able to buy such cards for the *kana* and the *kanji,* and he can make his own for the vocabulary and *bunkei* in this text. (Cutting a 3×5 index card into four equal parts will provide the blanks.) Always carry a pack of 50 or so with you. Look at one side, then say what is on the other without turning it over. Review these cards while riding a bus, shaving, or waiting for your lover to make her (his) belated appearance. Go through a new pack daily, then review all periodically. In the case of the *kana* and *kanji* cards, there is a danger, however, that I must acquaint you with. The author once carried the *kana* and *kanji* cards in his pocket and practiced writing these ideographs in the air with the tip of his finger as he strolled through a U.S. town. People who saw him suspected he was certifiable and urged that he be institutionalized. It was a humiliating experience, so don't practice your *kanji* on the streets of countries where ideographs are unknown but do practice with all the cards at every other opportunity.

Lesson Three

A.) Nouns
B.) Negatives of *Desu* and *Arimasu*
C.) The *ko, so, a,* and *do* words
D.) The uses of *no*

Useful Everyday Expressions

O-yasumi-nasai

Good night. This derives from the verb *yasumu,* meaning to rest. Adding *-nasai* to the verb stem makes it a polite imperative. The initial *o* is honorific. Thus, Please go to your honorable rest.

Arigatō (gozaimasu)

Thank you. *Ari* is the stem of the verb *aru,* to be, and *-gatō* is from *katai,* difficult. *Gozaimasu* is the polite form of *arimasu.* This means, literally, It is difficult to be. We can interpret this more loosely as, Such kindness (as you have shown me) is rare, or in more fanciful words, It is difficult for me to continue to exist after having been overwhelmed by such kindness. This is background only for those interested, as the author is, in word origins. Sometimes knowing the etymology will implant a word or phrase more deeply in the student's memory. *Gozaimasu* may be omitted when speaking to equals or inferiors. *Gozaimasu* refers to a present act (of kindness). The past tense *gozaimashita* should be used for past acts.

Sō desu ka.

Is that so? *Sō ka* would be rough and distinctly masculine. *Sō?* is largely feminine. *Sayō desu ka* is very polite and rather literary in tone. *Sō kai* is a variation of *Sō ka.* All mean, Is that so?

Dō itashimashite

You are welcome. *Dō* is the adverb how, while the second word derives from *itasu,* a polite equivalent of *suru* meaning 'to do.' Literally, 'how doing', but this makes little sense in English. Better think of this rather formal expression as meaning, Why are you saying such a thing (as thanks) when

31

I have done nothing to deserve it? More simply, 'Don't mention it' or 'Not at all.' 'Don't mention it' and 'It is really not worthy of your notice' are perhaps better translations than "You are welcome," since *Dō itashimashite* is sometimes said in response to praise. *Eigo ga hontō ni umai desu ne.* (Your English is really good) may elicit the response *Dō itashimashite*. Obviously, the translation 'You are welcome' would be inappropriate. 'Don't mention it' or 'Not at all' would be more fitting. When praised, you should deny any such merit or be rather vague and say, *Ē, mā, nan to ka....* or Yes, well, somehow (I manage to get by...)

Keep in mind that the Japanese usually deny any praise with vigor, except among close friends.

Note: When a clerk in a store thanks you for your patronage, it would not be appropriate to say *Dō itashimashite* to him in reply.

O-negai shimasu.

I beg of you. It has been said cynically that if foreigners living in Japan learn only this expression and use it continually, they will have gone far down the path to successful relations with the Japanese. *Negau* is the dictionary form of the verb meaning to ask for, to aspire, to beg, to wish for. The initial *o* is honorific, as it usually (but not always) is. *Shimasu* is the polite form of *suru*. *Kudasai* (please give me) is often replaced by this locution. Thus, instead of *O-mizu wo kudasai* (Please give me water), we may say, *O-mizu wo o-negai shimasu.* (I beg water of you.) A political candidate riding through the streets in a loudspeaker truck can be heard repeating, *"O-negai shimasu! O-negai shimasu! O-negai shimasu!"* ad nauseum. If you visit your son's school to plead with the principal to be lenient with your son for poking his teacher in the eye with a sharp stick, you should end your eloquent plea with innumerable bows and a dozen repetitions of *O-negai shimasu.* (Each repetition weakens Japanese resistance.) If you get in a taxi and want to go to the Ginza, you could tell your driver, *Ginza ni itte kudasai* (Please go to the Ginza) and be understood and delivered, but it would be more natural to say, *Ginza made o-negai shimasu.* (*Made* means 'as far as.')

Sumimasen.	I am sorry; Please forgive me; Thank you; Excuse me. Surely one of the most often heard words in Japanese. Women, who use this word more often than men, may say it without the first *m,* i.e., *su-imasen. Sumu* means 'to end,' so *sumimasen* means, It does not end. That is, My obligation to you does not end here. Actually, it is better not to use this word to superiors, but in the early stages of your Japanese studies, you need not concern yourself with such niceties. *Ai-sumimasen* means the same but is more emphatic.
Shirimasen or *Wakarimasen* or *Sā...*	*Shiru* is the verb to know; *shiranai* is the plain negative present tense. *Shirimasen* is its polite negative present, meaning I do not know. *Wakaru* is the dictionary form of the verb to understand. *Wakaranai* is the plain negative present while *Wakarimasen* is its polite equivalent, meaning I do not understand. While similar to 'know' and 'understand' in English, these words are not exactly the same, and their differences should be described to the learner early in his studies.

First, be aware that the Japanese will often say *wakarimasen* (I don't understand) when an English speaker would have said, I don't know. *Wakarimasen* means that one does not understand something even though the knowledge necessary to that understanding has been placed before him. *Shirimasen,* however, means that one does not know something because he has not had a chance to come face to face with that knowledge. The former can be taken to mean that the fault belongs to the speaker. The latter shifts the blame to someone else.

As might be expected, the Japanese often prefer to put the blame on their own shoulders and so say *Wakarimasen* more than *Shirimasen*. A clear instance of this is in the classroom where the student who doesn't know an answer will say *Wakarimasen* rather than *Shirimasen*. Had he said *Shirimasen,* he would be raising the dreadful suspicion that the teacher had neglected to provide the class with the material in which the answer was to be found.

Shirimasen can be used when the speaker has no particular obligation to know the answer to a question and when no fault is attached to not knowing. You might ask a friend if he knows anyone in a certain cosmetics manufacturing company in the town of Dazaifu on Kyushu. If your friend doesn't know anyone (and has no particular reason to know anyone) there, he can reply *Shirimasen* with perfect equanimity. If this is all too complicated, just say, *Sā...* which means 'Well...' and expresses the meaning of either *Wakarimasen* or *Shirimasen* as well as reflecting the Japanese proclivity for indirect vagueness.

Vocabulary

suru	the verb to do. Polite form is *shimasu.* Very often used because it can be added to many nouns to make them verbs. Thus, *shimpai* is the noun for worry; *shimpai suru* is the verb, to worry.
shiokara	salted fish guts
dai-kōbutsu	a favorite dish
shiru	to know
o-ushi	bull
me-ushi	cow (when one must distinguish gender)
ko-ushi	calf
onna-no-ko	girl (judging from *ko-ushi* above, *ko-onna* would seem more logical, but not so)
itasu	the polite form of *suru.* Used only about oneself or one's inner circle.
ochikomu	to fall into (from *ochiru,* to fall, and *komu,* to enter)
isogashii	busy
ikura	how much
hoshii	desired, desirable. Used with a gerund to mean, I want you to—Thus, *yasunde hoshii* (I want you to rest).
yasumu	to rest, go to bed
mae	before, in front of
biiru	beer

kau	to buy (*kai* is the verb stem)	*shokutaku*	dining table
ii	good, all right, OK, nice, fine	*soba*	side
		karakau	tease, rib
Eigo	English (language)	*yōsu*	conditions, appearance
ryokan	(Japanese-style) inn (tricky to pronounce)	*mō*	again, already, soon, now
sayō	so, such, like that (older form of *sō*)	*muzukashii*	difficult
		fuhai tanku	septic tank
okāsan	(your) mother	*sā*	well, come now
otōsan	(your) father	*ichido*	once, one time
hito	person, people	*asameshi*	breakfast
ware-ware	we (formal)	*Nihongo*	Japanese
oya	parent, parents	*nanji*	what time
takai	expensive, tall	*yukkuri*	slowly
yasui	cheap	*ara*	oh my, dear me
taihen	very	*motto*	more
daiji (na)	important. *Daiji na hon* is an important book.	*kudasai*	polite imperative of verb *kudasaru*, to give. Alone, it means Please give me— Following gerund, it adds 'please' to meaning of verb.
mizu	water		
Gōshū,	Australia		
Gōshū-jin	Australian		
dekiru	to be able to do (*dekimasu* is polite)	*nezake*	nightcap (from *neru*, to sleep, and *sake*, rice wine)
kanojo	she, her		
otoko-no-ko	boy		
mure	herd, group, crowd, flock, pack, bevy, swarm, cluster, gaggle	*chotto*	just a moment (also used to call for service, as in a restaurant)
obāsan	grandmother		
jidōsha	car, automobile (moves-by-itself-vehicle)	*fujin*	lady
		kata	person (polite)
		katagata	people (polite)
shako	garage	*ushi-oi*	cowboy
baka-yarō	idiot, foolish guy (horse-deer-fellow)	*umi*	sea, ocean
		unagi	eel
senkyōshi	missionary	*ushi*	cow, cattle
nigō-san	mistress	*iu*	to say. *Itte* is gerund. *Itta* is past tense (plain).
tokei	watch, clock		
tanoshii	pleasant, happy, enjoyable		
		shigoto	work, job
nyōbō	(my) wife	*oboeru*	remember, learn

negau	desire, wish for	*wakaru*	to understand.
made	as far as		*Wakarimasu* is po-
-nasai	see *O-yasumi-nasai*		lite form of *wakaru*.
	under Everyday Ex-		*Wakarimasen* is
	pressions above.		negative.
gozaimasu	Politer equivalent of		
	arimasu.		

Pattern Sentences

(Bunkei)

1. *Hakodate wa doko desu ka.* Where is Hakodate?
2. *Kono baka-yarō!* You idiot!
3. *Sochira no yōsu wa dō desu ka.* How are things (conditions) at your place? (lit., in that direction?)
4. *Biiru wo kai ni itta no wa donata desu ka.*
   Who went to buy beer?
5. *Mō ichido itte kudasai.* Please say it once more.
6. *Mō ichido o-negai shimasu.* Once again, please.
7. *Nanji desu ka. What time is it?*
8. *Motto yukkuri itte kudasai.* Please say it more slowly.
9. *Kore wa nan desu ka.* What is this?
   Yasui tokei desu. It is a cheap watch.
10. *Wakarimasu ka.* Do you understand?
    Iie, wakarimasen. No, I do not understand.
11. *Sā, muzukashii deshō.* Well, it will be difficult.
    (Actually, this is understood to mean, It is probably impossible.)
12. *Ara, obāsan wa mata fuhai-tanku ni ochikomimashita yo.*
    Dear me, grandmother has fallen into the septic tank again!
13. *Chotto sumimasen ga...* Excuse me for a moment (but)...
14. *Eigo ga dekimasu ka.* Can you speak English?
15. *Boku wa Gōshū-jin de wa arimasen.* I am not an Australian.
16. *Dō shimashita ka.* What happened? (Lit., How did you do?)
17. *Ii desu ka.* Is it all right?
    Ii desu. It is all right.
18. *Isogashii desu ka.* Are you busy?
    Sore wa kekkō desu. That is fine.
19. *Ikura desu ka.* How much is it?

20. *Doko desu ka.* Where is it?
    Koko wa Ginza desu ka. Is this the Ginza?
21. *Kō shite hoshii.* I want you to do it this way.
    (Lit., This way—doing—desired.)
22. *Ano ryokan wa taihen takai desu.* That inn is very expensive.
23. *Daiji na hon wa kinō no ryokan ni arimasen deshita.*
    (The important book was not in the inn (where I stayed) yesterday.)
    (Lit., Important book—yesterday's inn—was not there.)
24. *Dono ryokan ni aru deshō ka.* I wonder in what inn it is?
25. *Nihongo wo oboeru no wa asameshi-mae no shigoto de wa arimasen.*
    Learning Japanese is not an easy task. (Lit., Learning Japanese is
    not a job to be done before breakfast.)
26. *Soto wa sonna ni samui desu ka.* Is it as cold as all that outside?

How to Use

Nouns

Japanese is blessed by an absence of words like 'a,' 'an,' and 'the' preceding nouns. The absence, however, makes it almost impossible for its speakers to master the use of those three devilish words in English. *Unagi,* therefore, can be an eel or the eel. *Hanzai* can be a crime or the crime.

The basic forms of nouns do not change because of masculine, feminine, or neuter gender and they have no singulars or plurals. Thus, *ushi* can be a cow or the cow; it can be one cow or a thousand head; it can be a bull or a cow or a calf. (An *ushi-oi* is a cowboy, lit., a cow-chaser.) Distinctions are made by prefixes, not by changing the basic word *ushi. O-ushi* is a bull, *me-ushi* is a cow, and *ko-ushi* is a calf.

If we must emphasize the plurality of a noun like *ushi,* we can say *takusan no ushi* for lots of cattle or *gotō no ushi* for five head of cattle or *ushi no mure* for a herd of cattle.

In nouns for animate beings and in pronouns (more about these in the lesson on pronouns), the plural condition can sometimes be indicated by a suffix. Note these:

oya	parent (or parents)
oya-tachi	parents
kodomo	child (or children)
kodomo-ra	children
kodomo-tachi	children
fujin	lady (or ladies)
fujin-gata	ladies
sensei	teacher (or teachers)
sensei-tachi	teachers
sensei-gata	teachers (more polite than *sensei-tachi*)
seito	pupil (or pupils)
seito-tachi	pupils
seito-ra	pupils

There are a few nouns for animate beings in which the plural form is represented by a repetition of the word itself.

hito	person (or persons)
hito-bito	persons (The initial *h* in the second half of the word undergoes a phonetic change to *b* in *-bito.*)
kata	person or persons (lit., that direction)
kata-gata	persons [Again, the *k* becomes *g* (*-gata)* because of a phonetic change.]
ware-ware	we (*ware-ware* is formal but often heard.)

Negatives of *Desu* and *Arimasu*

The negative form of *desu* (which is really a contraction of *de arimasu)* is *de wa arimasen* (or *de arimasen).*

Present tense	*de wa arimasen*	is not, am not,
	(de wa nai)	are not

Past tense	*de wa arimasen deshita* *(de wa nakatta)*	was not, were not
Future conjectural	*de wa arimasen deshō* *(de wa nai darō)*	may not be
Conditional	*de wa arimasen nara* *(de wa nakereba)*	if there is not, if there are not,
Past Conditional	*de wa arimasen deshita* *nara (de wa nakatta* *nara)*	if there was not, if there were not,
Probable past	*de wa arimasen deshita* *deshō* *(de wa nakattarō)*	there probably was not, there probably were not
Gerund	*(de wa nakute)*	there not being

The words in parentheses above are the plain equivalents.

The student should note that *de wa* can be and often is contracted to the slightly less elegant and more colloquial *ja*. Thus, *de wa arimasen* becomes *ja arimasen; de wa nai* becomes *ja nai.*

De wa nai ka becomes *ja nai ka*. Both are translated as isn't it? aren't they? didn't they? aren't you? and so forth.

Hontō no koto wo itta ja nai ka.   (I) told the truth, didn't I?
    *(Hontō no koto=*truth's 'thing')
Ii nja nai ka.   It's all right, isn't it?

The negative forms of *arimasu* are as follows:

Present tense	*arimasen (nai)*	(there) do not exist, (I, we, you) do not have
Past tense	*arimasen deshita* *(nakatta)*	(there) did not exist, (I, we, you) did not have
Future conjectural	*arimasen deshō (nai* *darō* or *nakarō)*	(there) may not exist, (I, we, you) may not have.
Conditional	*arimasen deshitara*	if there is not, if there are not, if (I, you, we) do not have

The plain forms are given in parentheses.

Take note of the words *gozaimasu* and *gozaimasen,* which are even more polite forms of *arimasu* and *arimasen* and will be examined later.

40

The *ko, so, a,* and *do* words

Relating to	ko	so	a	do
person, people	kochira this person	sochira that person	achira that person over there	donata who
object	kore this	sore that	are that over there	dore which (of more than two things)
places	koko here kokora, kokorahen around here	soko there sokora, sokorahen around there	asoko[1] over there asokoira, asokorahen around over there	doko where
directions	kochira, kotchi this way, here	sochira, sotchi that way, there	achira[3] atchi[2] over there, over that way	dochira where which way dotchi which (of two things)
demonstrative adjectives	konna, kō iu this kind of of kono (ryokan) this (inn)	sonna, sō iu that kind of sono (ryokan) that (inn)	anna ā iu that (even more distant) kind of ano (ryokan) that (inn) over there	donna, dō iu what kind of dono (ryokan) which (inn)
adverbials	konna ni like this, as this kō this way	sonna ni like that, as that sō that way	anna ni like that, as that (more distant) ā that way	donna ni as what dō what way

[1] May also be pronounced as *asuko.* [2] *Atchi kotchi* means here and there.
[3] *Achira kochira* means here and there.
[4] *Konna, sonna,* and *anna* are often used with a contemptuous connotation:
Konna yasupikamono wa irimasen. (I don't want a cheap bauble like this.)

When the student studies the above, he will see that the words beginning with *ko* refer to things or persons near the speaker (this girl next to me). The *so* words are about middle-distance objects or the vicinity of the person being spoken to or about (that girl near you.) The *a* words are about people or things still farther off, close to neither the speaker nor to the person being spoken to or about (that girl we both ogled last Saturday). The *do* words are interrogative in nature.

All these adjectives, adverbs, nouns, and pronouns are in frequent use and should be learned quickly.

The student will see from the above that the Japanese often refer to a person as a "direction." Thus, the above *sochira* can mean that direction, you, your home, your family, or even your country.

Most importantly, you should accustom yourself to the four sounds 1) *ko,* 2) *so,* 3) *a,* and 4) *do.* When you meet them, think of them as 1) near-at-hand, 2) middle-distance, 3) farther off, and 4) interrogative.

The Uses of *No*

This small word has a bewildering variety of uses. We will undertake to explain most of them here and demonstrate how they are used in the *bunkei.*

a. *No* is a particle used to show possession. In this usage, *no* can be given as 's or as the preposition 'of.' *Tatsutaka-san no nezake,* therefore, can be Tatsutaka's nightcap or the nightcap of Tatsutaka's. Japanese has no direct equivalents of her, his, our, their, or my. These meanings must be expressed by adding *no* ('s) to the basic form of the pronoun: she, he, we, they, or I.

b. In English, we can show the physical relation of two nouns with a preposition: fish *in* the sea. In Japanese, we would say *umi no sakana,* meaning fish of the sea or the sea's fish. (This is not to gainsay such expressions as *Umi ni iru sakana* or Fish that are in the sea.) Another example would be *shako no jidōsha;* the garage's car or the car in the garage. Or we may say *Taiwan-jin no okusan,* which can mean the wife of the Taiwanese or a Taiwanese wife.

The general rule is that a noun that describes another noun will precede the noun described and will be followed by *no.* (*Sensei no biiru*=the teacher's beer.)

c. *No* is often the first word in many adverbial phrases of position:

Shokutaku no ue ni arimasu.	It is on top of the dining table.
Shokutaku no shita ni arimasu.	It is under the dining table.
Shokutaku no soba ni arimasu.	It is beside the dining table.

d. *No* can have the meanings of the 'fact that' and the 'person who.' Consider this sentence: *Shiokara wo tabete iru no ga hontŏ ni anata no obāsan desu ka.* (Is the person eating salted fish guts really your grandmother?) *Tabete iru* means 'is eating,' and *ga,* as we have seen, follows the immediate subject of the sentence. Thus, *no* stands for the 'person who.' *Onna-no-ko wo karakau no ga tanoshii desu.* (*Onna-no-ko* is girl; *karakau* is to tease; *tanoshii* is pleasant, delightful.) Here, the *no* cannot mean the 'person who.' If it did, this sentence would become, The person who teases girls is delightful. In this instance, then, the *no* means the 'fact that,' and this sentence becomes, The fact (or the act) of teasing girls is delightful.

e. *No* can also mean, 'It is a fact that...' when it precedes *desu.* Consider the sentence, *Nyōbō wa itsumo nete iru no desu.* (It is a fact that my wife is always sleeping.) We could also say, *Nyŏbō wa itsumo nete iru* or My wife is always sleeping, but the addition of *no desu* (it is a fact that) is more formal and slightly ameliorates the strongly assertive impact of the sentence ending in *nete iru.*

f. A confusing use of *no* occurs in this instance:

> *Senkyōshi no nigō-san*

Senkyōshi is a missionary, while *nigō-san* is a mistress. Thus, the above can mean either 'The missionary's mistress' or the mistress who is a missionary.' You will have to rely on context to tell the difference.

Likewise, *gakusei no tomodachi* can mean the student's friend or the friend who is a student.

g. *No* is often used by women in place of the interrogative particle *ka*.

Mō iku no. (Are you going already?)
The above *no* is spoken with a slightly rising inflection. In reply, you can use this same *no* but with a downward inflection:

Ē, gakkō ni iku no. Yes, I'm going to school.
This declarative *no* is used by women and children or by adult men when speaking to children.

h. *No,* followed by *desu* (or *da*) carries the sense of should or ought to. *Hayaku okiru no desu.* (You should get up early.) This is in addition to the usage under e. above.

Cultural Sidelights:

*** *Nigō-san* is written 'two—number—Mrs.' (Mrs. Number Two). She is, of course, the mistress, i.e., the woman who is usually the second ranking woman in a man's life. (In terms of actual affection, however, she may rank highest, since Japanese men often marry to carry on the family line but take mistresses for romance.) *Sangō-san* would be Mrs. Number Three; *Yongō-san* would be Mrs. Number Four. In these days of rising costs, not many Japanese men need to be able to count as high as five or six, though there was a recent news story about a Japanese businessman in Thailand who was alleged to have been feeding and loving eleven mistresses. (In the eyes of many Japanese men, he became an instant folk hero.)

*** The adjective *muzukashii* means difficult, but the Japanese often use it to mean impossible, which would sound too harsh to Japanese ears. Therefore, when the student hears *muzukashii,* he should first consider that it may mean, No, it can't be done.

*** *Isogashii* means busy, and being busy is a highly desirable state in Japan. In the U.S., for example, when a man says he is very

44

busy, he may well be commisserated with by his friends. ("Oh, that's too bad!") In Japan, however, being busy means that you are working, and if you are working, you are surviving. Centuries of hardship have conditioned the Japanese to think this way, despite recent affluence.

*** *Wakaru* is the verb, to understand. In Japan, it sometimes means more than mere comprehension of words. It may well mean agreement with the other person's position. (If you understand what I said, how can you *not* agree with my position?)

*** *Eigo ga dekimasu ka.* Can you speak English? Bear in mind that when English ability is part of a Japanese person's job (hotel clerk, travel guide, interpreter, teacher, et al), you should never make him lose face by casting doubt on that ability.

Study recommendations:

Suppose you are building a shed. The more nails you hammer into the boards, the stronger your shed will be, the better it will withstand typhoons. Your shed is the Japanese language. Your nails are Japanese words and pattern sentences. Each time you use one is like driving one more nail into a board. One or two nails won't do this job. It may take ten or twenty. To be really safe, you may want to hammer in fifty or even a hundred nails. Each time you use a word or a *bunkei,* the stronger your structure becomes, so use them often, whenever the occasion arises. In fact, you should go out of your way to arrange situations in which you can use such words. If you are trying to memorize several words for various Japanese dishes, steer the conversation around to food in Japan: what you like (*shiokara* or salted fish guts?) and don't like *(suki-yaki?),* how much rice your friend eats daily, what is her *dai-kōbutsu* (favorite dish)?

Lesson Four

A.) Names of nations, languages, and peoples

B.) The two classes of adjectives

Useful Everyday Expressions

Chotto matte kudasai.   Please wait just a moment. *Chotto* is 'just a moment' and *matte* is the *-te* form of the verb *matsu,* to wait (e. g., the gerund).

Kekkō desu.   That's fine. In Lesson One, we have seen that *kekkō* is an adjective meaning splendid, fine, good, excellent. One of Japan's most tattered proverbs is: *Nikkō wo miru made kekkō to iu na.* Or, Don't use the word splendid *(kekkō)* until you have seen (the Tokugawa mausolea at) Nikko. The student should note, however, that *Kekkō desu* seems to have contradictory uses. If offered a third serving of sweet bean-jelly laced with snake blood, you might well say *Kekkō desu,* to mean you don't want any more. On the other hand, if you want to accept an invitation to drinks and dinner at the cozy apartment of a genuine Kyoto *maiko* (I should be so lucky!), you could also say, *Kekkō desu,* meaning, Why, that's a simply splendid idea! In truth, there is little contradiction. In the former case, what you would actually be saying is, I'll get along fine without the bean-jelly. One way to distinguish between the two is to use *Iie, kekkō desu* in the negative sense and *Kekkō desu ne* in the affirmative.

Go-kurō-sama deshita.   Thank you for your trouble. The *go* is honorific; *kurō* means trouble or hardship; *sama* is honorific; *deshita* is the past tense of the copula *desu.* An often used expression. Take care, however, about using it to a superior or when something is done for you out of pure kindness. It is more commonly said to bellboys, maids, delivery men, and drivers.

45

Dōzo o-hairi kudasai.	Please come in. *O* is honorific and *hairi* is the stem of the verb *hairu,* to enter.
Dōzo	Please (when inviting a person to do something)
Ikaga desu ka.	How about it? How are you? (Lit., How is it?) The question, How are you?, is not asked as often or as casually in Japanese as in English. *Ikaga desu ka,* therefore, is posed more when you haven't seen the other person in a very long while or when there is a good reason to be concerned about his health. (For instance, if you know he was recently hospitalized.) *Ikaga desu ka* is used more in the first sense: How about it? At day's end, you might say to a coworker, "Let's go have a beer. *(Biiru wo nomi ni ikimashō).* How about it? *(Ikaga desu ka.)"*
O-genki desu ka.	Are you well? This is how you should inquire after a friend's health. Even so, it is not an automatic question, and you would not direct it at someone who appears in good health and whom you had met only the day before.
O-kage-sama de (genki desu.)	Thanks, I'm fine. This is how you would answer the question above. Lit., Thanks to your honorable shadow, (I'm in good health.) Although *O-kage-sama* means Thanks to you, it is often used in situations where the other party had no conceivable connection with whatever it was the speaker succeeded in doing. Bukichi may congratulate you on your recent successful wooing of a certain Nichigeki dancer, to which you could answer, *O-kagesama de...* (Thanks to you...) Actually, however, it was not Bukichi's pleas that inspired her surrender but rather it was candy or liquor—or a small box of *name-kuji* (seaslug)—that won the day. In such cases, what you are saying when using this phrase is that you are grateful for all the support everyone has given you in all fields, including Bukichi's friendship, over the years. Or *O-kage-sama de...* may mean merely Thanks for asking.

Vocabulary

A Adjectives

asai	shallow
hikui	low, short (of stature)
erai	great, celebrated, remarkable
karui	light
karai	hot (peppery)
amai	sweet
semai	narrow
shitashii	intimate
sukunai	few
surudoi	sharp
tadashii	correct
usui	thin
wakai [1]	young
yasashii	gentle, easy
yoroshii	all right
ōi	many, lots, numerous
kuwashii	detailed
mijikai	short
kurushii	trying, painful
kurai	dark
osoroshii	frightening
otonashii	mild, well-behaved
sabishii	lonely
ayashii	strange, suspicious
kayui	itchy
kitanai	dirty
nagai	long
atarashii	new
oishii	delicious
omoshiroi	interesting, pleasant
tōi	far
samui	cold
atsui	hot or thick
utsukushii	beautiful
suzushii	cool
shiroi	white
kuroi	black
kitsui	tight (as with clothes), strict
kanashii	sorrowful
urayamashii	enviable
yurui	loose (as with clothes)
mezurashii	unusual
furui	old

B Adjectives followed by na

rikō	intelligent, clever
fushizen	unnatural
kantan	simple
shitsurei	rude
shizuka	quiet, calm, slow
hen	odd
yūmei	famous
hitsuyō	necessary
shinsetsu	kind
suki [2]	liked, pleasing
kirai	disliked, hateful
dame	no good
iya	disliked
baka	foolish
byōki	sick
jōzu	skillful
heta	unskillful, poor at
shōjiki	honest
jūbun	enough
taikutsu	boring
suteki	wonderful
hima	free (in the sense of time)
busahō	rude

B Adjectives followed by *no*

hontō	truthful	*igai*	unexpected
uso	untruthful	*hisashiburi*	appearing after a
yohodo	a considerable		long time
wazuka	a slight	*tada*	free of charge
taitei	most	*takusan*	many
sukoshi	a little	*tekitō*	proper
minna	all (the)	*tokubetsu*	special
chotto	a small	*jūyō* ³	important
atarimae	proper, right, obvious		

Adjectives that are both A and B

kiiroi	*kiiro no*	yellow	*chiisai*	*chiisa na*	small
ōkii	*ōki na*	large	*okashii*	*okashi na*	strange, funny

ı Describes youthfulness from the teens and beyond. Under that age, *chiisai* (small) is used instead.

2 pronounce as *ski*

3 This adjective can also be followed by *na*.

Pattern Sentences

(Bunkei)

1. *Hontō no koto wo itte kudasai. Uso wa kirai desu.* Please speak the truth. I don't like lies.
2. *Anata no utsukushii hisho ni aitai.* I would like to meet your beautiful secretary.
3. *Taitei no Indo-jin wa Eigo ga dekimasu.* Most Indians can speak English.
4. *Ashi no hayai otoko ga kachimasu.* The fast man wins.
5. *Shiroi shatsu ga arimasu ka. Kono shatsu wa akai desu.* Do you have a white shirt? This shirt is red.
6. *Minna no sensei wa Itaria-go ga wakarimasu ka shira.* I wonder if all the teachers understand Italian? (Note that the use of *ka shira* in place of just *ka* introduces the meaning of 'I wonder if...' *Ka shira* is used mostly by women but men may use it too when talking to younger women or to much younger people in general.
7. *Hitori mo wakarimasen.* Not a one understands.

8. *Sore wa okashii hanashi desu ne.* That's odd, isn't it.

9. *Taikutsu na eiga wo mite chotto no aida nemurimashita.* Watching a boring movie, I fell asleep for a little while.

10. *Ano yasashii Tai-jin wa takusan no okane wo motte imasu.* That gentle Thai has lots of money.

11. *Sono Roshia-jin wa hontō ni heta na Nihongo wo hanashimasu ne. Mimi ga itai yo.* That Russian really speaks poor Japanese, doesn't he? My ears hurt.

12. *Sono Doitsu-jin no kutsu wa akakute, sono Furansu-jin no kutsu wa shiroi desu.* That German's shoes are red, and that Frenchman's shoes are white.

13. *Kitanai hanashi wa iya. Yamete kudasai.* I don't like dirty stories. Please stop.

14. *Fuirippin no kokugo wa nan desu ka. Eigo desu ka. Supeingo desu ka. Iie, Tagarogugo desu.* What is the national language of the Philippines? Is it English? Is it Spanish? No, it is Tagalog.

15. *Kuroi zubon ga arimasu ka.* Do you have any black trousers?

16. *Kono zubon wa kuroi desu. Haite kudasai.* These trousers are black. Please try them on.

17. *Um. Chotto kitsui desu ne.* Hmm. They are a little tight, you see.

18. *Ano machi ga sonna ni tōkereba ikanai hō ga ii darō.* If that town is that far, it would probably be better not to go.

How to Use

The Two Classes of Adjectives

The two kinds of Japanese adjectives have elsewhere been given several different (and confusing) names, but here we will opt for the simplest description: A adjectives and B adjectives.

A Adjectives

An A adjective functions like an adjective in English, e.g. it precedes the noun it modifies (*atsui hi* or a hot day), but it can also serve as a verb. While meaning hot as in *atsui hi, atsui* can also be 'is hot,' as in: *Kyō wa atsui.* (Today—as for—is hot.)

All A adjectives end in the letter *i*. This can be expanded to say that all A adjectives end in *ai, ii, ui,* or *oi.* Note, however, that they never end in *ei.*

Fortunately for the student, the A adjectives do not have first, second, or third person forms nor do they have singulars or plurals. Thus, the word intelligent *(kashikoi)* as in 'I am intelligent,' 'You are intelligent,' 'She is intelligent' does not change.

Examples of A adjectives are:

akai	red	*takai*	tall/ costly
chikai	near	*yasui*	cheap
hayai	fast/ early	*itai*	painful
osoi	slow/ late	*fukai*	deep

The past tense positive of all A adjectives is easily formed by dropping the final *i* and substituting *katta*. Thus, the past tense of *chiisai* (small) becomes *chiisakatta*. However, this past positive form can only be used as a verb, e.g., *Sono hako wa chiisakatta*. (That box was small.) We cannot say *chiisakatta hako* for a 'box that was small.'

The present tense negative of A adjectives is constructed by substituting *ku* for the final *i* (*hayai* becomes *hayaku*) and adding *nai* or *arimasen* (see Lesson Two). *Hayaku nai* (or *hayaku arimasen*) means not fast or not early. The past tense negative is formed in the same way by using *nakatta* in place of *nai* and *arimasen deshita* in place of *arimasen*.

When the final *i* of the A adjectives is dropped, you may add *-kereba* to form the conditional, that is, if or when . . . or add *-na-kereba* for the negative.

samukereba	when it is cold
samukunakereba	when it is not cold
shirokereba	if it is white
shirokunakereba	if it is not white
osokereba	if it is late
osokunakereba	if it is not late

Or, instead of *-kereba*, you may add the conjectural *-karō*, meaning It probably will be . . .

Samukarō.	It probably will be cold.
Samukunakarō.	It probably won't be cold.
Shirokarō.	It probably is white.
Shirokunakarō.	It probably isn't white.
Osokarō.	(He, she, it) will probably be late.
Osokunakarō.	(He, she, it) probably won't be late.

The A adjectives have what is known as a *-te* form, with *-kute* being substituted for the final *i*. Thus, the adjective for lukewarm, *nurui,* becomes *nurukute,* while the word for bad, *warui,* becomes *warukute.* This *-te* form is used, for instance, when two (or more) adjectives are said together: This shirt is soft and warm. [*Kono shatsu wa yawarakakute atatakai (desu).*] It is also used in an adjective that is the final word in a non-final clause within a sentence: That car is expensive, and I cannot buy it. *(Sono jidōsha wa takakute kau koto ga dekimasen.)* Note the absence of the pronoun before *kau.*

By replacing the final *i* of an A adjective with *ku,* then following that with *naru* (to become), we have:

Sabishiku narimashita. *(natta).*	(I) became lonely.
Masshiroku narimashita. *(natta).*	(It) became pure white.
Chiisaku narimashita. *(natta).*	(It) became small.

The idea of excess can be built into any true adjective by adding *-sugiru* (to be too much, to go too far) to the adjective's stem, e.g., the A adjective without its final *i. Tsuyoi* for strong becomes *tsuyo-sugiru* or too strong. *Omoi* for heavy becomes *omo-sugiru* or too heavy. *Sugiru* is a verb and can be so conjugated, i.e., *Sugita, sugimasu, suginai, sugimasen, sugimashō,* and so forth.

A adjectives can be created by suffixing *-rashii* (like, appears to be) to many nouns. Add *-rashii* to *otoko* (man) and get *otoko-rashii* (manly).

> *Onna-rashii* — womanly
> *Kodomo-rashii* — childish
> *Baka-rashii* — foolish

-rashii can even be attached to adverbs, *sō-rashii* (it seems to be so) and to other A adjectives, to wit, *takai-rashii* (it seems to be tall/costly).

See the *bunkei* below for usage of the above.

In this lesson we have met *tanoshii* (pleasant, cheerful), *kanashii* (sorrowful), and *taikutsu na* (boring). Remember when you employ these adjectives, they should be referring to your own emotions—not those of another.

B Adjectives

The B adjectives have also been called quasi-adjectives, adjectival nominatives, and adjectival verbs, but we will call them B adjectives. A major difference between B and A adjectives is that the B's do not conjugate. For instance, *kirei* (pretty, nice) can never be changed to *kire-, kireku-, kireku-nai,* or what have you. It must always be *kirei.*

The roots of B adjectives are quantitative nouns or adverbs and compound words that were originally Chinese. *Takusan* (much, many) is an example of the former while *gūzen* (accidental) is typical of the latter.

When the B adjectives precede and modify a noun, they are invariably followed by *na* or *no.* By replacing *na* or *no* with *-sugiru,* you can introduce the meaning of 'too (much)' as with the A adjectives. (See above.)

shizuka na	quiet	*iroiro no*	various
teinei na	polite	*tekitō no*	proper
kokkei na	humorous	*jōtō no*	excellent
daiji na	important	*tokubetsu no*	special

Many of these adjectives can become adverbs (e.g. *teinei ni* is politely) when *ni* is used in place of *na* or *no*. More about this in the chapter on adverbs.

While the roots of many of the B adjectives are nouns, it is usually no longer possible to use them as nouns. There are a few exceptions, such as the noun *shizen* (nature), the adjective *shizen no* (natural), and the adverb *shizen ni* (naturally). Thus, *Kanojo wa shizen wo ai shite imasu* (She loves nature).

There is no rule to tell the student whether one of the B adjectives is followed by *na* or *no*. You must consult a dictionary or educated native speaker and memorize the correct usage.

Because these adjectives do not conjugate, they are followed by a copula, that is, a form of the verb 'to be:'

Kanojo wa kichigai desu.	She is crazy.
Haha no kotoba wa uso ja arimasen deshita.	Mother's words were not a lie.

Note that neither *no* nor *na* is needed between the B adjective, e.g., *kichigai,* and the copula (*desu*).

When two B adjectives are used together, they should be separated by the particle *de,* which is a contraction of *desu*.

Otaku no kodomo wa rikō de sunao desu ne. Your child is intelligent and obedient, isn't (she)?

When three B adjectives are used together, it is advisable to insert *sono ue* (and, on top of that) between the second and third.

Otaku no kodomo wa rikō de sunao de sono ue kirei desu, ne. Your child is intelligent, obedient, and, on top of that, pretty, isn't (she)?

The B adjective *onaji* or *onnaji* (same) is irregular. Used before a noun, it is not followed by *no* or *na*. Otherwise, its functions are the same as other adjectives in this class.

Other B adjectives are unstable and cross the line between A and B, as noted above. That is, we can say *ōkii uchi* or *ōki na uchi* for a big house and *yawarakai makura* or *yawaraka na makura* for a soft pillow. Also, *chiisai jidōsha* or *chiisa na jidōsha* for a small car and *okashii hanashi* or *okashi na hanashi* for a funny (or strange) story. Some can be followed by either *na* or *no: jūyō no hanashi* or

Names of nations, languages, and peoples

	Country (Kuni)	Language (Kotoba)	People (Hitobito)
Japan	Nihon (or Nippon)	Nihon-go	Nihon-jin
China	Chūgoku	Chūgoku-go	Chūgoku-jin
Soviet Union	Soren (or Roshia)	Roshia-go	Roshia-jin
America	Amerika	Eigo	Amerika-jin
England	Eikoku Igirisu	Eigo Eigo	Eikoku-jin Igirisu-jin
Thailand	Tai	Tai-go	Tai-jin
Pakistan	Pakisutan	Pakisutan-go	Pakisutan-jin
India	Indo	Hinzu-go Urudu-go Bengaru-go	Indo-jin
Malaysia	Marēshia	Marē-go	Marēshia-jin
Indonesia	Indoneshia	Indoneshia-go	Indoneshia-jin

jūyō na hanashi for an important talk. When confronted with these irregularities, make the best of the situation and memorize the correct usage.

(See the *bunkei* below.)

Cultural sidelights:

*** *Suki* ranges in meaning from mild fondness to deep love. A Japanese man may use this word to express how he feels about

(continued)

	Country (Kuni)	Language (Kotoba)	People (Hitobito)
Philippines	Fuirippin	Tagarogu-go	Fuirippin-jin
France	Furansu	Furansu-go	Furansu-jin
Holland	Oranda	Oranda-go	Oranda-jin
Germany	Doitsu	Doitsu-go	Doitsu-jin
Mexico	Mekishiko	Supein-go	Mekishiko-jin
Taiwan	Taiwan	Chūgoku-go	Taiwan-jin
Norway	Norue	Norue-go	Norue-jin
Greece	Girisha	Girisha-go	Girisha-jin
Italy	Itaria	Itaria-go	Itaria-jin
Spain	Supein	Supein-go	Supein-jin
Sweden	Sueden	Sueden-go	Sueden-jin
Denmark	Denmāku	Denmāku-go	Denmāku-jin

both *kimosui* (eel liver soup) and about his bride. Although his heart may burn with love for his wife, he avoids excessive declarations of his feelings. *Omae ga suki da.* (I like you) may be about as far as he is prepared to go. When he proposed marriage, he may have contented himself with a casual sentence like, *Omae no mendō wo mitai.* (I'd like to look after you.)

*** *Erai* usually means great in the sense of illustrious and celebrated. These days, many Americans have taken to using 'great' for a much broader range of meanings—wonderful, pleasing, enjoyable, delicious, et al—but the Japanese have not expanded the usage of *erai* to that extent. Praised be God.

*** *Baka* is a fool, and *baka na* is foolish. It is written with the two *kanji* for horse and for deer, and a horsedeer might well appear to be foolish. It is a common and rather mild reproof. Although there are a good many ways to traduce a person's intelligence or appearance in Japanese, the Japanese do not make as much use of them as we do, theirs not being a confrontational society like the American. *Baka* is about as much as many of them are willing to say.

Study recommendations:

It is natural for students of Japanese to turn for help to any handy native speaker of the language, no matter who that speaker may be. In many instances, this is justifiable. Even a kindergarten pupil should be able to help you pronounce the word for rice *(gohan)* correctly. As we move farther along with our language studies, however, we may mistakenly look for help from persons not qualified to give it. We should, therefore, try to seek such assistance from college graduates, remembering that graduate engineers in Japan may have a grasp on their own tongue that is no firmer than the grasp most American engineers have on English. On questions of language, I am sorry to say, some foreigners cleave to the advice of char-women, bar hostesses, taxi drivers, and neighborhood children like Holy Writ. Try not to fall into this trap.

Lesson Five

Kana

Most foreign students of Japanese begin their studies with the spoken language, which may be more immediately useful to them than the written. In my case, I had one and a half years of full-time study of the spoken word before being thrown into the fray with the written. Even Japanese children, obviously, have four or five years of exposure to the spoken before tackling the written.

Perhaps God, in his Infinite Wisdom, so ordained it, remembering what a Jesuit missionary in Japan reported to Rome in the 17th century. This man of God wrote home that the Japanese language must have been devised by Satan to prevent the teaching of the Gospel to heathens in Japan. Confronting the foreign student with both written and spoken Japanese simultaneously and in equal dosages might, therefore, be classed as cruel and unusual treatment.

Learning Japanese is not so devilishly hard, of course, but I believe we should let the student ease his way into an amiable liaison with the *kana* and *kanji* only after first learning some of the spoken language. If, therefore, you have absorbed the first four lessons herein, you should be ready to tackle the *kana* syllabaries (syllabary: a set of phonetic characters each of which represents a syllable). Then you can proceed, apart from the regular lessons, to work with the *kana* at your own pace, activated by the urgency of your own need to come to grips with the written language.

Later on in this text, we will begin to look at several *kanji* in each lesson. Therefore, by the time you finish the first volume, you could—depending on your own exertions—know both syllabaries as well as fifty or so of the most often used *kanji*.

Although you still will not be able to read a newspaper, you should at least have an appreciation of the philosophy behind the *kanji* and *kana* and enough knowledge to read some signs, headlines, and names. This smattering will also facilitate your study of the spoken tongue in ways we will demonstrate later. Subsequent volumes will increase the pace so that by the end of the third volume, the student should know the 1,005 *Kyōiku Kanji* (Educational *Kanji*) with their main readings and one or two or three important compounds. These are the *kanji* that Japanese pupils must learn during their nine years of compulsory education. (The *Tōyō Kanji* or *Kanji* in Daily Use number 1,945—those that are needed to read a newspaper.)

Let us now consider how the *kana* syllabaries came into being and then, how to make them part of your linguistic armamentarium.

Even several centuries after the birth of Jesus Christ, the Japanese still had no written language. For a race as intelligent as the Japanese are, this is astounding, considering how much earlier the cultures on the Mediterranean rim were able to record their deeds. Then, as Chinese visited Japan (and as Japanese went to China), the Chinese script gradually became known to certain classes in the land the Chinese knew as Wa.

The people of Wa learned, for instance, how to write the Chinese character *(kanji)* for 'bridge'. Of course, they already had a spoken word for bridge *(hashi),* so they called the *kanji* from China *'hashi'* or they attempted to imitate the native Chinese pronunciation of that character. Since there were three major Chinese dialects and many minor ones, the vocalization of the character by the Japanese varied with the native province of the Chinese teacher instructing them.

Even then, the problem of how to keep written records was not wholly solved for the Japanese. Whereas the Chinese could convert all their spoken words into ideographs, the Japanese could use them only with their native nouns and the stems of verbs and adjectives. In Japanese, there were sounds—verb conjugations, adjectival endings, names, and particles—that had no equivalents in Chinese. To solve the dilemma of how to put these purely Japanese names, words, and word endings on paper, the people of Wa came up with what was—at least, initially—a rather awkward solution. They decided to assign sounds arbitrarily to certain Chinese characters, without regard to meaning.

This was awkward because the arbitrarily selected *kanji* probably were written with five or ten or more strokes each. Let's say, then, that a Japanese wanted to write what he would have said as *Atarashikatta no desu* (It was new.) He would first have penned 新, the *kanji* with the meaning of 'new,' and then the *seven* 'sound' characters, each of which might have been as complicated and time-consuming to pen as 新 itself. It became a classic case of the tail far outweighing the dog.

Patently, these characters *(shi-ka-tsu-ta no-de-su)* used only for their sound value had to be simplified. In the fullness of time, this was done and by about the ninth century, the Japanese had two simplified sets of symbols, either of which they could use to record all the sounds in their language. Indeed, Japan's (as well as the world's) first novel—the *Genji Monogatari*—was written in the 11th century by the Lady Murasaki Shikibu entirely in *kana*.

Of the two syllabaries, *hiragana*—a cursive adaption of the 'sound' *kanji*—is used much more today than *katakana* and is learned in school first. The *hiragana* flows like long-hand while the *katakana* is stiff and angular, more like printing. *Katakana* is reserved for loan words (words adopted from foreign languages), telegrams, foreign names, and onomatopoetic words. Sometimes, a writer will also write a purely Japanese word in *katakana* when it is a colloquialism or when he wishes to emphasize it—by making it stand out from the surrounding *hiragana*.

Katakana or ('side *kana*') is so called because its simplified form usually consists of just one 'side' or element of the original *kanji,* which was chosen for its sound. The *katakana* symbol リ *(ri),* for instance, is the right side of its parent: 利

Generally, Japanese *kana* as well as *kanji* are written from left to right and from top to bottom. Bearing this in mind, the student is asked to learn their stroke order first. It is vital that this be done first, before mistaken stroke orders learned haphazardly become set

Hiragana (Syllabary) Chart

a	i	u	e	o	ya	yu	yo
あ a	い i	う u	え e	お o	や ya	ゆ yu	よ yo
か ka	き ki	く ku	け ke	こ ko	きゃ kya	きゅ kyu	きょ kyo
が ga	ぎ gi	ぐ gu	げ ge	ご go	ぎゃ gya	ぎゅ gyu	ぎょ gyo
さ sa	し shi	す su	せ se	そ so	しゃ sha	しゅ shu	しょ sho
ざ za	じ ji	ず zu	ぜ ze	ぞ zo	じゃ ja	じゅ ju	じょ jo
た ta	ち chi	つ tsu	て te	と to	ちゃ cha	ちゅ chu	ちょ cho
だ da	ぢ ji	づ zu	で de	ど do	ぢゃ jya	ぢゅ ju	ぢょ jo
な na	に ni	ぬ nu	ね ne	の no	にゃ nya	にゅ nyu	にょ nyo
は ha	ひ hi	ふ fu	へ (h)e	ほ ho	ひゃ hya	ひゅ hyu	ひょ hyo
ば ba	び bi	ぶ bu	べ be	ぼ bo	びゃ bya	びゅ byu	びょ byo
ぱ pa	ぴ pi	ぷ pu	ぺ pe	ぽ po	ぴゃ pya	ぴゅ pyu	ぴょ pyo
ま ma	み mi	む mu	め me	も mo	みゃ mya	みゅ myu	みょ myo
ら ra	り ri	る ru	れ re	ろ ro	りゃ rya	りゅ ryu	りょ ryo
わ wa				を wo			ん n

in mental concrete. Charts in this chapter will teach you the stroke order.

Try to obtain *genkō yōshi* (manuscript paper) or line off your own paper in small squares. Practice writing the *kana,* in their correct stroke order, in those squares. After you have written each one several hundred times, the stroke order will begin to come naturally, and the *kana* symbols themselves will be putting down roots in your memory.

Also, make small cards with the *kana* on one side and the *rōmaji* (the Roman letters) on the other. Carry a pack of these cards for frequent and ready use.

The *kana* syllabaries will accompany the stroke order charts

Hiragana Stroke Order

Ka-na	Stroke No. #1 #2 #3 #4	Rō-maji	Ka-na	Stroke No. #1 #2 #3 #4	Rō-maji	Ka-na	Stroke No. #1 #2 #3 #4	Rō-maji
あ	⁻ ナ あ	a	た	⁻ ナ た た	ta	ま	⁻ ⁼ ま	ma
い	ı い	i	ち	⁻ ち	chi	み	み み	mi
う	⁻ う	u	つ	つ	tsu	む	⁻ む む	mu
え	⁻ え	e	て	て	te	め	＼ め	me
お	⁻ お お	o	と	ヽ と	to	も	し も も	mo
か	ヮ か か	ka	な	⁻ ナ な	na	や	つ や や	ya
き	⁻ ⁼ き	ki	に	｜ に に	ni	ゆ	｜ ゆ ゆ	yu
く	く	ku	ぬ	＼ ぬ	nu	よ	⁻ よ	yo
け	｜ け け	ke	ね	｜ ね	ne	ら	⁻ ら	ra
こ	⁼ こ	ko	の	の	no	り	｜ り	ri
さ	⁻ さ	sa	は	｜ に は	ha	る	る	ru
し	し	shi	ひ	ひ	hi	れ	｜ れ	re
す	⁻ す	su	ふ	ぅ ふ ふ	fu	ろ	ろ	ro
せ	⁻ せ せ	se	へ	へ	(h)e	わ	｜ わ	wa
そ	⁻ そ	so	ほ	｜ に ほ	ho	を	⁻ を を	wo
						ん	ん	n

herein. The best way to master these is to write them over and over, either on paper or in the air with your forefinger. If you live in Japan or in a Japanese environment abroad, you will have more frequent opportunities to see the *kana* in use around you, on signs and in newspapers. Otherwise, you should arrange to buy children's books written entirely or mostly in *kana*. Also, for younger readers, are to be found books with the *kana* (called *furigana* or *rubi*) printed alongside the *kanji* to tell learners how to read the *kanji*. These would give you practice in reading both the *kana* and the *kanji*.

To the first fifteen symbols in each syllabary have been attached tiny arrows to show the direction in which the stroke is made. (Again,

Katakana (Syllabary) Chart

a	i	u	e	o	ya	yu	yo
ア a	イ i	ウ u	エ e	オ o	ヤ ya	ユ yu	ヨ yo
カ ka	キ ki	ク ku	ケ ke	コ ko	キャ kya	キュ kyu	キョ kyo
ガ ga	ギ gi	グ gu	ゲ ge	ゴ go	ギャ gya	ギュ gyu	ギョ gyo
サ sa	シ shi	ス su	セ se	ソ so	シャ sha	シュ shu	ジョ sho
ザ za	ジ ji	ズ zu	ゼ ze	ゾ zo	ジャ ja²	ジュ ju	ジョ jo
タ ta	チ chi	ツ tsu	テ te	ト to	チャ cha	チュ chu	チョ cho
ダ da	ヂ ji	ヅ zu	デ de	ド do	ヂャ jya²	ヂュ ju	ヂョ jo
ナ na	ニ ni	ヌ nu	ネ ne	ノ no	ニャ nya	ニュ nyu	ニョ nyo
ハ ha	ヒ hi	フ fu	ヘ (h)e	ホ ho	ヒャ hya	ヒュ hyu	ヒョ hyo
バ ba	ビ bi	ブ bu	ベ be	ボ bo	ビャ bya	ビュ byu	ビョ byo
パ pa	ピ pi	プ pu	ペ pe	ポ po	ピャ pya	ピュ pyu	ピョ pyo
マ ma	ミ mi	ム mu	メ me	モ mo	ミャ mya	ミュ myu	ミョ myo
ラ ra	リ ri	ル ru	レ re	ロ ro	リャ rya	リュ ryu	リョ ryo
ワ wa				ヲ wo			ン n
ファ fa¹	フィ fi¹		フェ fe¹	フォ fo¹			

¹ 4 syllables that appear only in 'loan words'

² Essentially, *ja* and *jya* are the same sound.

they are almost always left to right and top to bottom.) Thereafter, the student should be able to write each stroke in the correct direction without the assistance of these marks.

Just as we have the a,b,c alphabetical order in English, so there is a proper order for the *kana* as shown in the charts: *a, i, u. e, o, ka, ki, ku, ke, ko,* and so forth. Become familiar with this order in the course of your studies. Entries in Japanese dictionaries are arranged accordingly, as are names in telephone directories. Without knowing

Katakana Stroke Order

Ka-na	Stroke No. #1 #2 #3 #4	Rō-maji	Ka-na	Stroke No. #1 #2 #3 #4	Rō-maji	Ka-na	Stroke No. #1 #2 #3 #4	Rō-maji
ア		a	タ		ta	マ		ma
イ		i	チ		chi	ミ		mi
ウ		u	ツ		tsu	ム		mu
エ		e	テ		te	メ		me
オ		o	ト		to	モ		mo
カ		ka	ナ		na	ヤ		ya
キ		ki	ニ		ni	ユ		yu
ク		ku	ヌ		nu	ヨ		yo
ケ		ke	ネ		ne	ラ		ra
コ		ko	ノ		no	リ		ri
サ		sa	ハ		ha	ル		ru
シ		shi	ヒ		hi	レ		re
ス		su	フ		fu	ロ		ro
セ		se	ヘ		(h)e	ワ		wa
ソ		so	ホ		ho	ヲ		wo
						ン		n

that order, it would be most difficult to use those dictionaries and directories.

Several important notes about *kana* usage:

1. To form a long vowel in *hiragana*, the *kana* or the last letter in the Romanized syllable is added in the case of *a, i, u,* and *e.* For instance, to elongate *ka*, you attach the *kana* for *a*, making it *kā*. To elongate *yu*, attach the *kana* for *u*, making it *yū*. *O*, however, may be an exception. Any syllable (or *kana*, that is) ending in *o (ko, so, to, ho, no, ro)* can be converted to a long vowel by the addition of *o* or *u: to* is written either *to* and *o* (と お) or *to* and *u* (とう).

2. In *katakana,* however, the long vowel is more simply made: a vertical line is drawn below the *katakana* to be elongated. Shown horizontally, this would be テーブル for *tēburu* (table).

3. In the section on pronunciation, we discussed the double consonant, as in *zutto* (meaning all the way, all the time) and *makka* (bright red). In *hiragana, zutto* would be ずっと. You will see that the first *t* is expressed by the *kana* for *tsu* (つ) and is usually written a little smaller than the preceding and succeeding *kana.* The same is true of *ya* (や), *yu* (ゆ), and *yo* (よ) in the diphthongs such as *hya* (ひゃ), *myo* (みょ), *nyu* (にゅ), *mya* (みゃ), and *ryu* (りゅ). Refer to the charts.

4. Three anomalies should be pointed out. These are the post-positions *e, o* or *wo,* and *wa. E* is used to express direction, e.g., *machi e iku* (to go to town). One might expect that the *e* would be written with the *hiragana* え or the *katakana* エ, but instead, it is written へ (same in *hiragana* and *katakana.*)

The postposition indicating the accusative case—that is, following a direct object—is shown in *rōmaji* as *wo* or *o* (depending on the preference of the text's author) and the *kana* for *o* (お or オ) might be expected. Instead, を or ヲ (for *wo*) is used.

The third and last exception is the postposition *wa* following the remote subject of a sentence. Generally, *wa* is, of course, わ or ワ, but here we have to use は or ハ (for *ha*).

5. In the charts you will see, to the right and just above certain of the phonetic symbols, the small diacritical marks ゛ and ゜. The former are the *dakuon,* but we will call them the 'two dots.' The latter are the *han-dakuon,* which we will call the "single circles." Both are more commonly called *nigori* and *maru* in Japanese.

As shown in the charts, these modify the sound of the symbol, whereby *ka* (か) with ゛ becomes *ga* (が) and *hi* (ひ) with ゜ becomes *pi* (ぴ).

God bless.

(For supplemental study, I recommend the following two books:
EASY HIRAGANA, by Fujihiko Kaneda
EASY KATAKANA, by Tina Wells
Both are published by YOHAN Publications, Inc., Tokyo.)

Lesson Six

A.) Conjugation A Verbs
B.) *-masu*
C.) Periods of Time

Useful Everyday Expressions

Moshi moshi Hello. Used on the telephone. Also, when trying to get someone's attention, usually from a distance.

Dochira e? Where are you going?

O-dekake desu ka. Are you going out? *O* is honorific and *dekake* is the stem of the verb *dekakeru* (to go out). Said to anyone leaving his home or office.

Dōzo yoroshiku... Loosely, Please treat me kindly. Standard greeting when being introduced to someone. Short for *Dōzo yoroshiku o-negai shimasu.* Even more casual is '*Yoroshiku...*' alone.

De wa, mata... Lit., 'Well then, later...' In effect, 'See you later.' Breezy in tone.

Vocabulary

kotoba	word	*kūki*	air
mono	thing(s), both physical & abstract	*ame*	rain
		ashi	leg, foot
koto	thing (abstract), 'it'	*hana*	flower
inu	dog	*asa*	morning
tomodachi	friend	*ima*	now
kusuri	medicine	*hashi*	chopsticks
gakkō	school	*shōsetsu*	novel
kimono	Japanese-style dress	*mado*	window
niku	meat	*heya*	room
shimbun	newspaper	*niwa*	garden
yasai	vegetable	*uchi*	house
kawa	river	*atama*	head

65

denwa	telephone	*yama*	mountain
mise	store, shop	*yuki*	snow
tegami	letter	*te*	hand
zasshi	magazine	*sora*	sky
ki	tree	*satō*	sugar
fukanō	impossible	*sakura no hana*	cherry blossom

Pattern Sentences

(Bunkei)

1. *Sakura no hana ga saite imasu.* The cherry blossoms are blooming.
2. *Koko wa nan no gakkō desu ka.* What school is this? (*Nan* is the elliptical form of *nani.*)
3. *Mainichi sakana wo taberu hito wa kono heya ni imasu ka.* Is there a person in this room who eats fish daily?
4. *Sora wo tonde iru mono wa nan deshō ka.* What is that thing flying in the sky?
5. *Chūgokujin no tomodachi ga katta kara ureshii desu.* Since my Chinese friend won, I am happy.
6. *Yama ni yuki ga futte imasu.* Snow is falling in the mountains.
7. *Nihonjin wa sakana ga suki desu ga niku wo amari tabemasen.* The Japanese like fish but do not eat much meat.
8. *Abunai kara oyoganaide kudasai.* Because it is dangerous, please do not swim.
9. *Kyō no shimbun wo yomimashita ka.* Have you read today's newspaper?
10. *Hashi de yasai wo tabemasu.* (I) eat vegetables with chopsticks.
11. *Senshū uchi no inu wa kusuri wo nonde genki ni narimashita.* Last week our dog drank the medicine and recovered (lit., became healthy).
12. *Onna no ko wa tegami wo yonde nakimashita.* The girl cried after reading the letter.
13. *Ano kusai mono wo hayaku dase!* Put that smelly thing out quickly!

14. *Kon'ya kodomo ga nakeba utatte kudasai.* If the child cries tonight, please sing (to it).

15. *Nani mo iwanai hito wa dare desu ka.* Who is the person who says nothing? (*Nani mo* is 'nothing.')

16. *Ano shōsetsu wo yonde warawanakatta no wa hontō desu ka.* Is it true that you read that novel and did not laugh?

17. *Kyō gakkō wo yasumimasu.* I will not go to school today. Lit., I will 'rest' school today. Note that whereas 'to rest' *(yasumu)* is intransitive in English, it functions as a transitive verb in Japanese.

How to Use
Verbs

Before taking up the conjugation A verbs, a few words about verbs in general:

Japanese has no exact equivalent to the English infinitive. What is used instead is the so-called dictionary form of the verb or the form in which verbs are listed in lexicons. The English infinitive 'to know' would be *shiru* (I know, I will know) in Japanese. Because this form can be present or future tense, it might well be called the 'non-past.' The dictionary form always ends in *u.*

Where we would say, "I want to know," the Japanese would express this desire by adding *-tai* to the verb stem, e.g., *shiri-tai.* Where we would say, "To know all is impossible," the Japanese would say *koto* after the dictionary form of the verb, e.g. *Nan de mo kan de mo shiru koto wa fukanō desu* (*Nan de mo kan de mo* is 'Anything and everything'.)

It should come as a relief to know that verbs have no person or number. Give thanks for small favors.

In English we place the adverb 'not' before a verb to express negation. ("I do *not* know.") In Japanese the suffix *-nai* is added to the negative stem of the verb for this purpose. *Shiru* (know), whose negative stem is *shira-,* becomes *shiranai* (not know).

As in English, Japanese verbs can be either transitive or intransitive, e.g. they may or may not take direct objects, but a few verbs may be both transitive and intransitive. Further, verbs that are transitive in English may be intransitive in Japanese. *Au* (meet or fit), *noru* (ride), and *hairu* (enter) are examples of these. We say 'ride a horse,' whereas the Japanese say 'ride on a horse' *(uma ni noru)*. We say 'enter a house,' whereas the Japanese say 'enter into a house' *(ie ni hairu)*.

In the case of most verbs, the potential, causative, and passive voices are made by certain verb endings and can be conjugated like regular verbs.

Almost all verbs are regular and are classed in one of two conjugations: A and B. The two major exceptions are the irregular verbs *kuru* (to come) and *suru* (to do), while *iku* (to go) is slightly irregular. These will be described farther on.

Conjugation A Verbs

The two charts in this chapter show stems of A verbs as well as tell you how to form their gerunds and plain past tenses.

Twelve Conjugation A verbs (both transitive and intransitive) are listed in the first chart. There are, of course, many more. Here is a sampling:

Transitive		Intransitive	
oku	to place	*tsuku*	to arrive
umu	to give birth to	*teru*	to shine
fuku	to clean off, wipe	*naru*	to become
kasu	to lend	*furu*	to fall (as rain)
utau	to sing	*suwaru*	to sit (in the Japanese style)

In the next chapter, conjugation B verbs will be discussed. Invariably, B verbs end in *-iru* or *-eru*. However—and here's the rub—certain A verbs also end in *-eru* or *-iru*. Take, as an example, *negiru* (to bargain). If it were a B verb, its basic stem would be *negi-*. Being an A verb, however, the stem is *negiri-*.

Is there a way to tell the difference? Not easily. When you have mastered the *kana* (and some *kanji*), you can look up verbs in question in a *jisho* (dictionary) like Kenkyusha's Japanese-English dictionary (my vade mecum) and you will find example sentences showing whether it is *negi-* or *negiri-*. (Kenkyusha's example is *Daibu negitta ue...* or, After much haggling....The past tense *negitta* shows the stem to be *negiri-*. Were the stem *negi-*, the past tense would have been *negita*.) Till then you should remember the examples given below.

Conjugation A Verbs Ending in:

-eru			*-iru*		
heru		to decrease	*mairu*		to come or go
neru	"	knead	*hashiru*	"	run
shaberu	"	chatter	*kiru*	"	cut
suberu	"	slip, slide	*ijiru*	"	fiddle with
keru	"	kick	*kagiru*	"	be limited (to)
shimeru	"	become damp	*nigiru*	"	grasp

Please note the following about the first chart, "Conjugation A Verbs:"

The dictionary form of the verb has already been explained. *Aruku* can mean 'I walk' or 'I will walk' or 'I (always) walk,' as in answer to the question, "How do you get to the office every morning?" In fact, the one word *aruku* can constitute a complete sentence in Japanese. If asked, "Are you going to walk or ride the horse?" you might answer merely, *"Aruku."* ("I will walk.") The subject of the predicate is understood to be "I" (unless, of course, another person is under discussion), in which instance a different form of the verb such as *arukareru* or *o-aruki ni naru* might be used.

Conjugation A Verbs

Dictionary Form	(Basic) Stem -i	(Negative) Stem -a	Plain Imperative -e	Conditional Stem -e	Suggestive or Conjectural -ō
aruku (walk)	aruki-	aruka(nai) aruka(nakatta)	aruke	aruke(ba)	arukō
shinu (die)	shini-	shina(nai) shina(nakatta)	shine	shine(ba)	shinō
naku (cry)	naki-	naka(nai) naka(nakatta)	nake	nake(ba)	nakō
au (meet or fit)	ai-	awa(nai) awa(nakatta)	ae	ae(ba)	aō
warau (laugh)	warai-	warawa(nai) warawa(nakatta)	warae	warae(ba)	waraō
saku (blossom)	saki-	saka(nai) saka(nakatta)	sake	sake(ba)	sakō

Intransitive

Conjugation A Verbs (continued)

	Dictionary Form	(Basic) Stem -i	(Negative) Stem -a	Plain Imperative -e	Conditional Stem -e	Suggestive or Conjectural -ō
Transitive	kiku (ask, hear)	kiki-	kika(nai) kika(nakatta)	kike	kike(ba)	kikō
	kau (buy)	kai-	kawa(nai) kawa(nakatta)	kae	kae(ba)	kaō
	dasu (put out)	dashi-	dasa(nai) dasa(nakatta)	dase	dase(ba)	dasō
	ugokasu (move)	ugokashi-	ugokasa(nai) ugokasa(nakatta)	ugokase	ugokase(ba)	ugokasō
	motsu (have, hold)	mochi-	mota(nai) mota(nakatta)	mote	mote(ba)	motō
	narau (learn)	narai-	narawa(nai) narawa(nakatta)	narae	narae(ba)	naraō

The (Basic) Stem is the one that takes the polite endings *-masu, -mashita,* etc. (More about these later in this chapter.)

The (Negative) Stem takes the suffix *-nai* (plain present) and *-nakatta* (plain past) to make the verb negative.

Thus, the plain present negative form of *warau* (to laugh) is *warawanai* (see chart) while the plain past negative is *warawanakatta.* In the chart, the past tense is given under the present.

The student should note that the addition of *-ra* to any of these plain past negative forms makes them conditional:

	warawanakatta	(I) did not laugh
	warawanakattara	If (I) had not laughed
or,	*dasanakatta*	(I) did not put out
	dasanakattara	If (I) had not put out

The plain imperative is just what it says. *Aruke!* is the rough command ("Walk!"), complete in itself and almost military in tone. It is constructed by dropping the final *i* of the Basic Stem and replacing it with *e.*

This plain imperative also happens to be the conditional stem, which is, however, not complete in itself. It needs the addition of *-ba.* Thus, *aruke-ba* is, If (I) walk...*Kake-ba* is, If (I) write....

The final column in the chart shows the suggestive or conjectural. *Arukō* can be, Let's walk or (I) probably will walk. *Kikō* is, Let's listen or (I) will probably listen.

The second chart shows how to form the gerund and plain past tense of A verbs.

The gerund has several uses in Japanese. Followed by the verb *iru* or *imasu* (to be), it tells of an ongoing action, e.g. the progressive present, as in *Nani wo itte imasu ka* (What are you saying?) For the progressive past, change *iru* to *ita* or *imasu* to *imashita. Hana wa saite imashita (ita).* The flowers were blooming.

It can tell of a condition resulting from an action. *Kare wa uchi ni kaette imasu.* He has returned to the house (and is still there).

It shows a habitual action. *Kanojo wa maishū o-furo ni haitte imasu.* She bathes weekly. Lit., She enters the honorable bath every week. (... *o-furo ni hairimasu* would mean the same, but *haitte imasu* emphasizes the regularity of her ablutions.)

The gerund can also be the verb form ending a non-final clause within a sentence, carrying the force of 'and.' *Kesa okite kaisha ni ikimashita.* I got up this morning and went to the office. Lit., this morning... getting up... office...to... (I) went.

Within a sentence, a gerund followed by the word *kara* (lit., from) carries the meaning of 'after'. *Tsukue wo fuite kara Eigo wo benkyō shimashita.* After wiping off the desk, I studied English.

Note the ending *-ru* and its gerund taking *-tte*. In the next chapter, we see that verbs ending in *-ru*, e.g. (*-iru* or *-eru*), become gerunds by suffixing *-te* instead of *-tte:* a major difference between the A and B verbs.

If you say *kudasai* after a gerund, you get a very useful expression. *Hanashite kudasai* is Please speak. *Hashitte kudasai* is Please run. *Kitte kudasai* is Please cut. And so forth. *Kudasai* is the polite imperative form of the slightly irregular verb *kudasaru* (to deign to give, to deign to do), always used about the second or sometimes third person, never about yourself, except as recipient of the favor.

To express the negative with *kudasai,* just add *-de* (and then say *kudasai*) to the plain present negative of any verb. *Arukanai* (the negative stem *aruka-* plus *nai*) is, I do not walk, I will not walk. Add *-de,* then say *kudasai: Arukanai-de kudasai* is Please do not walk.

Warawanaide kudasai	Please don't laugh.
Kawanaide kudasai	Please don't buy.
Kikanaide kudasai	Please don't ask.

This works as well with the Conjugation B and the irregular verbs.

Note that a polite gerund can be constructed by the use of *-mashite.* This is added to the Basic Stem.

Machi e aruite ikimashite eiga wo mimashita.
I walked to town and saw a movie.

Usually, however, —*mashite* is not suffixed to verbs within the sentence.

Forming the Gerund and Plain Past Tense of Conjugation A Verbs

	If the verb is one whose dictionary form ends in—	To form gerund—	To form plain past tense—
	-bu, -mu, -nu	Substitute *nde* for *-bu, -mu,* or *-nu*	Substitute *-nda* for *-bu, -mu,* or *-nu*
Examples	*tobu* (fly) *yomu* (read)	*tonde* (flying) *yonde* (reading)	*tonda* (flew) *yonda* (read)
	-ku	Substitute *-ite* for *-ku*	Substitute *-ita* for *-ku*
Examples	*kiku* (hear, ask)	*kiite* (hearing, asking)	*kiita* (heard, asked)
	-gu	Substitute *-ide* for *-gu*	Substitute *-ida* for *-gu*
Examples	*oyogu* (swim)	*oyoide* (swimming)	*oyoida* (swam)
	-su	Substitute *-shite* for *-su*	Substitute *-shita* for *-su*
Examples	*dasu* (put out)	*dashite* (putting out)	*dashita* (put out)
	-tsu, -ru, -u (as a single syllable)	Substitute *-tte* for *-tsu, -ru,* and *-u*	Substitute *-tta* for *-tsu, -ru, -u*
Examples	*katsu* (win) *shiru* (know) *iu* (say)	*katte* (winning) *shitte* (knowing) *itte* (saying)	*katta* (won) *shitta* (knew) *itta* (said)

The column in the chart about the formation of the plain past tense should be self-explanatory.

A note about the past tense of verbs in an introductory subordinate clause: Suppose you wish to say, If she had not come this morning, I would have gone swimming. We might do it this way: *Kesa kanojo ga konakatta nara, oyogi ni ikimashita.* This would have been understood and would have been correct. However, a native speaker might just as well have said, *Kesa kanojo ga konakereba, oyogi ni ikimashita.* That is, the verb in the subordinate clause would be *konakereba* (if she does not come). What has happened is that the tense of the final verb *(ikimashita)* governs the tense of the earlier verb *kuru (konakereba)* and superimposes the past tense on it.

-masu

We have come across the suffix *-masu* before. Although it is actually a verb itself, it is used only when added to the Basic Stem of other verbs. It can be used in reference to any person and serves the purpose of making your speech polite (although there are even politer ways of saying the same thing). Its three main uses are demonstrated below with the A verb *oyogu* for to swim:

oyogimasu	(I) swim, will swim, do swim
oyogimashita	(I) swam, did swim
oyogimashō	Let's swim, (I) probably will swim

There are other forms that *-masu* can take, such as the gerund *-mashite* mentioned above, *-mase* or *-mashi* suffixed to *kudasai* to make it even politer, the conditional *-maseba* and *-mashitara,* and the repetitive *-mashitari.*

Periods of Time

Last	Today's	Next	Every
kinō no asa yesterday morning	*kesa* this morning	*ashita no asa* tomorrow morning	*maiasa* every morning
kinō no ban last evening also, *sakuban*	*komban* this evening	*ashita no ban* tomorrow evening	*maiban* every evening
kinō no yoru last night also, *sakuya*	*konya* tonight	*ashita no yoru* *myōban* tomorrow night	*maiyo* every night
kinō yesterday also, *sakujitsu*	*kyō, konnichi* today	*ashita, myōnichi* tomorrow	*mainichi, ichinichi goto ni* every day
senshū last week	*konshū* this week	*raishū* next week	*maishū, isshūkan goto ni* every week
sengetsu last month	*kongetsu* this month	*raigetsu* next month	*maitsuki, maigetsu, ikka-getsu goto ni* every month
kyonen, sakunen last year	*kotoshi* this year	*rainen* next year	*maitoshi, mainen* every year

Learn also: *ototoi*—day before yesterday
                ototoshi—year before last
                issakunen—year before last
                asatte—day after tomorrow
                myōgonichi—day after tomorrow
                goto ni—at intervals of

maijikan, ichijikan-goto ni every hour

This chart gives 47 expressions used to express periods of time: recent, present, future, and repetitive. They can be used at the beginning of the sentence, as in:

Raigetsu sakura no hana wa sakimasu ka shira.
I wonder if the cherries will bloom next month?

Or within a sentence:

Watakushi wa maitoshi atarashii jidōsha wo kaimasu.
I buy a new car every year.

In most instances, however, the Japanese use such words at the start of a sentence.

Cultural sidelights:

Under Useful Everyday Expressions, we find *O-dekake desu ka* and *Dochira e?* Both are ritualistic formulae. They are asked to strengthen social bonds, and the questioner usually has little genuine interest in knowing the answer. (To be sure, we could say the same about "How are you?" in English.) An appropriate response to *Dochira e?* would be, *Chotto sokorahen made...* (Just down the road a ways...)

Elsewhere, I have related the story of my landlady who invariably asked the first (above) question every morning when I approached the front door, coat on and hat in hand. At length, as I was stepping outside, the devil made me reply, *"Iie, kyō wa dekake-masen."* (No, I am not going out today.) Nonetheless, her response to even that never varied: *De wa, itte irasshai.* Well then, be on your way. Lit., Well then, please go and come back.

The forms of *-masu* are extremely important, since the student should nearly always attach them to the final verb in all his sentences during his early experiences with Japanese. He will hear the plain forms, e.g., verbs without the *-masu* endings, often and may wonder why they are forbidden to him. It is because there are many sensitivities and special circumstances involved, and it is safer to stick with *-masu* et al until he is aware of most of them. (What saves many foreigners from utter disaster in this area is that the Japanese—God bless 'em—will often forgive the newcomer all but the most heinous errors.)

Study recommendations:

Press ahead with your *kana* practice. Also, it is time for a review of Lesson One on pronunciation.

Lesson Seven

A.) Basic numbers
B.) Desiderative *-tai*
C.) Gerund + *hoshii*
D.) "and"
E.) Conjugation B verbs

Useful Everyday Expressions

O-namae wa?   What is your name? Lit., honorable—name—as for?

Shimizu Mieko to mōshimasu.
I am Mieko Shimizu. Lit., I say Mieko Shimizu. *Mōsu* means 'to say' and is used only about oneself. Of course, Miss Shimizu could also say just *Shimizu Mieko desu.*

Mata aimashō.   Let's meet again.

Osoreirimasu ga...   Would you oblige me by...? *Osoreiru* is a verb meaning to be overwhelmed with gratitude, embarrassment, or awe. This is a common expression used when asking for a favor.

Nani mo arimasen ga dōzo...
Please help yourself. Lit., there is nothing (to eat) but please... Said to a guest when you are the host.

Senjitsu wa dōmo...   Thanks for the other day. Lit., the other day—as for—very much. . .

Dōmo...   One of the most useful, though puzzling words in Japanese. Consult Kenkyusha's Japanese-English Dictionary to see the various meanings.* In the negative sense, it is used to suggest that you don't know an answer or that you have a contrary opinion about something but don't want to be succinct in expressing it. In another sense, *dōmo...* is an abbreviation for quite a few bromidic expressions: *Dōmo arigatō, Dōmo shitsurei*

---

* Very, somehow, and indeed are prominent among them.

78

shimashita, Dōmo o-jama shimashita, Dōmo o-kamai mo dekimasen de..., Dōmo o-sewa-sama deshita, and so on.

Dō ka shimashita ka. Is something wrong?

Wakatte imasu. Lit., I am understanding (it). Actually, this phrase conveys, I already know that, so there's no need to say more about it.

Tsuma wo go-shōkai shimasu.
  Let me introduce my wife.

Shikata ga arimasen. It cannot be helped.

Denwa bangō wo oshiete kudasai.
  Please tell (lit., teach) me your telephone number. You may substitute *jūsho* or *tokoro-banchi* (address) for *denwa bangō* (telephone number). This is more natural than asking, What is your telephone number? *(Denwa bangō wa nan desu ka.)*

Vocabulary

iro	color	*tsuma*	(my) wife (humble but formal)
kuchi	mouth		
soto	outside	*dōbutsu*	animal
hidari	left	*dojin*	native (also, *genjū-min*)
migi	right	*ochitsuku*	to be calm, become settled
kazoku	family		
yūhan	evening meal	*mekata*	weight (of an object)
nimotsu	luggage		
henji	answer	*taijū*	weight (of a person)
kita	north	*kiru*	to wear (in general)
minami	south	*haku*	to wear, put on (trousers or shoes)
nishi	west		
nioi	odor, scent	*zubon*	trousers
inaka	rural area	*mada*	yet, still
mochiron	of course	*tokoro*	place
oneisan	elder sister	*-en*	yen
oniisan	elder brother	*michi*	road
ojiisan	grandfather	*hirumeshi*	lunch
gaikoku	foreign country	*kaeru*	return (to where one belongs, e.g., home, office, or native land.)
gaikokugo	foreign language		
tsukau	to use		

kome (*o-kome*)	rice after it has been milled but before it has been cooked	*okane*	money (the *o* is polite.)
kaban	briefcase, suitcase	*kakaru*	to take time, hang, cost
higashi	east	*sebiro*	jacket, coat
omote	front (*ie no omote* is front of house)	*kaburu*	to wear, put on (a hat)
ura	rear (*ie no ura* is rear of house.)	*kisha*	(steam) train
		densha	(electric) train
asobu	to play, to be idle, to enjoy oneself	*tamago*	egg

Pattern Sentences

(Bunkei)

1. *Ichi kara ni-jū made kazoete hoshii desu.* I want you to count from one to twenty.

2. *Wakamono yo. Nishi ni ike.* Go west, young man. *Waka(i)* is young and *mono,* written with a different *kanji* than the one for 'thing,' means person. *Yo* is the spoken exclamation point.

3. *Jū-en wo kuremasu ka.* Will you give me ten yen?

4. *Kinō kita no yama ga yuki ni owaremashita.* Yesterday snow covered the mountains to the north.

5. *Benkyō ni akimashita.* I have grown weary of studying. *Mō takusan da.* I have had enough. (Lit., Already—plenty—is.)

6. *Kon'ya genjū-min wa ochitsuite imasen ne.* The natives are restless tonight, aren't they? (Lit., the natives are not calm tonight, are they?)

7. *Nimotsu wa futatsu deshita ka.* Did you have two pieces of luggage? *Iie, mittsu deshita.* No, it was three (that I had).

8. *O-kome wo kawanaide kudasai.* Please don't buy (any) rice. *Uchi ni mada aru kara...* We still have some at home... (Lit., In the house—still—is—because—)

9. *Hontō ni Kyōto ni asobi ni ikimasu ka.* Are you really going to Kyoto for pleasure? *Okane ga takusan kakarimasu yo.* It will cost a lot of money! (Note that the stem of any verb plus *ni* introduces the meaning of 'in order to.' Thus, *Sore wo ii ni kaetta* or I came back to say that.)

10. *Hayaku nigete kudasai.* Please flee quickly.

11. *Kurai tokoro ni hairitakunai desu.* I don't want to go into a dark place.
12. *Sebiro no iro wa nani ga suki desu ka.* What color jacket do you like? (Jacket's color—as for—what—like? Again, *wa* sets off the remote subject. That is, it shows that we are about to mention the color of jackets. Then we get down to specifics and ask what color you like.)
13. *Sono hyakushō wa kekkon shite imasu.* That farmer is married.

How to Use

Numbers

The father of the famous Meiji Era scholar Yukichi Fukuzawa once said to his son, "It is abominable that children should be taught the use of numbers—the instruments of merchants." I sympathize with the elder Fukuzawa and wish I could omit all mention herein of the wretched things, but this was not meant to be. Let us, therefore, face up to our duty and take numbers a little at a time.

First, we have the numbers taken from the Chinese:

ichi	one	*jū-ichi*	eleven
ni	two	*jū-ni*	twelve
san	three	*jū-san*	thirteen
shi (yon)	four	*jū-shi*	fourteen
go	five	*jū-go*	fifteen
roku	six	*jū-roku*	sixteen
shichi (nana)		*jū-shichi (jū-nana)*	
	seven		seventeen
hachi	eight	*jū-hachi*	eighteen
ku, kyū	nine	*jū-ku (jū-kyū)*	nineteen
jū	ten	*ni-jū*	twenty

hyaku	100
issen	1,000
ichi-man	10,000

hyaku-man	1,000,000
sen-man	10,000,000
ichi-oku	100,000,000

Use the above to count from one to twenty (and beyond): *ichi, ni, san, shi,* and so forth. They are also used in the formation of what are called numerators. Sadly, the Japanese do not count objects and creatures in the simple way we do in English: one car, six snakes, eight sheets of paper, two pencils, twelve battleships, or three girls. Instead, they combine these so-called Chinese numbers with 'counters' to form numerators. The counter for sheets of paper is *-mai;* that for cars is *-dai;* the one for houses is *-ken;* and that for people is *-nin.* Thus, one car is *ichidai no jidōsha,* three people is *sannin no hito-tachi,* and four houses is *yongen no uchi.*

These numerators can also be used after whatever is being counted, as in: *empitsu wo sampon motsu* (to have three pencils).

These numerators will be dealt with in detail later.

The construction of ordinal numbers is easy: add *-bamme* to the Chinese unit: *ichi-bamme* becomes first, *ni-bamme,* second, and *sam-bamme,* third. *Go-bamme no musume wa uchi no desu.* (The fifth girl is ours.)

Dai before the ordinal number is only for emphasis. *Dai-ichi-bamme* is still 'first,' only stronger. *Dai,* the equivalent of 'No.,' may precede the Chinese number, and *-bamme* may be omitted, so that *Dai-ichi* becomes No. One, *Dai-ni* is No. Two, and so on. We often come across such words as *Dai-ichi Hoteru* (No. One Hotel) and *Dai-ichi Ginkō* (No. One Bank).

You will see that some numbers carry two pronunciations, as *shi* or *yon* for four. *Yon* is often preferred to *shi,* since the latter is a reading of the *kanji* for death. In other instances, the alternate pronunciation may exist for phonetic convenience. For the present, learn both and use either one. In time, we will come to prefer one or the other and understand the reason for that preference.

There are also the so-called Japanese numbers, which go only as far as ten:

hitotsu	one	*muttsu*	six
futatsu	two	*nanatsu*	seven
mittsu	three	*yattsu*	eight
yottsu	four	*kokonotsu*	nine
itsutsu	five	*tō*	ten

These numbers can be used to count many different objects but never human beings. Some objects may not be blessed with proper numerators or the numerators may be obscure. In any event, you may use these until you learn the numerators, and they may be used either before or after the object being counted, although the latter has a slight edge in preference:

Yottsu no tamago wo kudasai.	Please give me four eggs.
Tamago wo yottsu kudasai.	Please give me four eggs.

The right numerator for eggs is *ko;* thus, *ikko* (written *ichi-ko*) *no tamago* (one egg), *niko no tamago* (two eggs), *sanko no tamago* (three eggs), and so forth. Whether you know the numerator or not, however, you may say *hitotsu no tamago, futatsu no tamago,* and so on, but you must never, never use the Chinese number alone, that is, without the numerator, to count things. You would never say *ichi no tamago* or *ni no tamago.* It must be either *hitotsu no tamago* or *ikko no tamago* for one egg.

You will sometimes hear the number one used in expressions where the speaker doesn't really mean just one:

*Ippai *nomimasen ka.*	Won't you have a drink?
*Ippuku *shimasen ka.*	Won't you take a breather? Lit., Won't you 'do' a puff (of tobacco)?

The speaker's intent here is not to limit his vis-a-vis to only one this or that but merely to start him off with one and carry on from there. (*Note the absence of the accusative marker *wo.* This is customary after numbers or numerators: *Sono zankoku na ryōshi wa* *sūhiki uchi-koroshimashita.* That cruel hunter shot and killed several (some kind of a four-legged animal).

Desiderative *-tai*

We have already seen that *-tai* added to the basic stem of a verb, e.g., *tabetai, ikitai, kaeritai,* introduces the meaning of desire: *ikitai* for 'want to go' and *tabetai* for 'want to eat.' (More about this usage under Cultural Sidelights in this chapter.)

Further, we have noted that the direct object of a verb is indicated (and followed) by the particle *wo.* A verb to whose stem *-tai* is suffixed, however, should—properly speaking—be separated from its direct object not by *wo* but by the particle *ga.* For instance,

> *Akai shitagi ga kaitai desu.*
> I want to buy red underwear.

In English, underwear is still the direct object, but in Japanese *shitagi* becomes, in effect, the immediate subject of the predicate *kaitai.* Again,

> *Nodo ga kawaita kara biiru ga nomitai desu.*
> Because I am thirsty (lit., my throat has dried), I want to drink beer.

These days, especially among the young, there is a tendency to replace *ga* with *wo* in such sentences.

To express the desire to go somewhere, the particle *e* or *ni* follows the word for the destination:

> *Uchi ni kaeritai desu.*
> (I) want to go home.
> *Kyūshū no inaka e ikitai desu.*
> (I) want to go to the rural districts of Kyushu.

-tai can be conjugated as a Class A adjective. That is, *-takatta* is the past tense.

Ikitai.	I wish to go.
Ikitakatta.	I wished to go.

-taku becomes the adverbial form:

Ikitaku omoimashita.	I thought I wanted to go.

To this form *-taku* are added *nai, nakatta* et al to make the negatives:

Ikitaku-nai.	I don't want to go.
Ikitaku-nai no desu.	I don't want to go.
Ikitaku-arimasen.	I don't want to go.
Ikitaku-nakatta.	I did not want to go.
Ikitaku-nakatta no desu.	I did not want to go.
Ikitaku-arimasen deshita.	I did not want to go.

-tagaru is like *-tai* in that it expresses a wish but there are three differences:

a. It is stronger in meaning.
b. It is used only about a third person
c. It is treated as a verb and not an adjective.

Kyō obāsama wa dare ni mo aitagarimasen.
    Today grandmother does not want to meet anyone.
Yasuchika-san wa kanojo ni aitagatte imasu.
    Yasuchika is very eager to meet her.
Uchi no kodomo-tachi wa daigaku ni ikitagarimasu.
    Our children want to go to college.

Gerund and *hoshii*

Saying *hoshii* (A adjective for desired or desirable) after a gerund results in the meaning of "I want that done."

> *Konya yasunde hoshii desu.*
> This evening (I) want (you) to rest.
> *Konya yasunde hoshikunai desu.*
> This evening (I) do not want (you) to rest.

In Chapter 5 there was a chart detailing the structure of the gerund with Conjugation A verbs. With Conjugation B verbs, however, the gerund is much more simple. In all cases, the final *-ru* of the dictionary form of B verbs is dropped and replaced by *-te:*

Meaning	Dictionary Form	Gerund
to praise	*homeru*	*homete*
to think	*kangaeru*	*kangaete*
to stop	*yameru*	*yamete*

Examples:
Kangaete kudasai. Please think.
Yamete hoshii. I want (you) to stop.
Homete hoshikunai. I don't want (you) to praise (me).

More about B verbs in this chapter.

"and"

In Japanese, there are several ways to express "and." Here, we will examine three:

1. *to*   "and" between nouns in a limited series.
2. *ya*   "and" between nouns in a unlimited series.
3. *sōshite*   "and" as a conjunction at the beginning of or within a sentence.

Examples: *Sebiro to zubon to kutsu ga kaitai desu.*
              (I) want to buy a jacket and trousers
              and shoes (and that is all).
            Sebiro ya zubon ya kutsu ga kaitai desu.
              (I) want to buy a jacket and trousers and shoes
              (and maybe some other things).
            Yūbe sebiro to zubon wo kaimashita.
            Sōshite kesa kutsu wo kaimashita.
              Last night I bought a jacket and trousers.
              And this morning I bought shoes.

The student should note that whereas in English we might say, "My wife wants diamonds, furs, perfumes, and a sports car," the Japanese would separate the nouns with the particle *to.* "*Kanai wa daiya to kegawa to kōsui to supōtsu-kā ga hoshii desu.*" (In the case of my own frau, she would probably use *ya* instead of *to,* preferring the bastinado to any form of restriction on her shopping list.)

Conjugation B Verbs

Together with Conjugation A verbs, those of the B Conjugation make up the main body of Japanese verbs. The B verbs end in either *-iru* or *-eru.*

B verbs ending in *-eru*

Transitive		**Intransitive**	
taberu	to eat	*haeru*	to grow, sprout
kangaeru	to think	*kotaeru*	to answer
nageru	to throw	*arawareru*	to appear
ageru	to give (to a superior or equal)	*kieru*	to disappear
akeru	to open	*kowareru*	to break, be broken

Conjugation B Verbs

Dictionary Form	(Basic) Stem	(Negative) Stem	Plain Imperative	Conditional Stem	Suggestive or Conditional	Plain Past Tense
	-e or -i	-e or -i	-ro or-yo	-re	-yō	-ta
deru (i. or t.) go out	de-	de (nai) / de (nakatta)	dero / deyo	dere (ba)	deyō	deta
hajimeru (t.) begin	hajime-	hajime (nai) / hajime (nakatta)	hajimero / hajimeyo	hajimere (ba)	hajimeyō	hajimeta
miseru (t.) show	mise-	mise (nai) / mise (nakatta)	misero / miseyo	misere (ba)	miseyō	miseta
wasureru (t.) forget	wasure-	wasure (nai) / wasure (nakatta)	wasurero / wasureyo	wasurere (ba)	wasureyō	wasureta
yameru (t.) stop	yame-	yame (nai) / yame (nakatta)	yamero / yameyo	yamere (ba)	yameyō	yameta
dekiru (i.) can do, is made	deki-	deki (nai) / deki (nakatta)		dekire (ba)	dekiyō	dekita
iru (i.) to be in a place*	i-	i (nai) / i (nakatta)	iro / iyo	ire (ba)	iyō	ita
nobiru (i.) to stretch out	nobi-	nobi (nai) / nobi (nakatta)	nobiro / nobiyo	nobire (ba)	nobiyō	nobita
okiru (i.) to get up	oki-	oki(nai) / oki (nakatta)	okiro / okiyo	okire (ba)	okiyō	okita
tariru (i.) to suffice	tari-	tari (nai) / tari (nakatta)		tarire (ba)	tariyō	tarita

* of all living creatures

homeru	to praise	*makeru*	to be defeated
ireru	to put in	*nagareru*	to flow
oshieru	to teach	*neru*	to sleep, go to sleep,
shimeru	to close		be in bed
kureru	to give (act performed		
	by another)	*nigeru*	to escape
kazoeru	to count	*deru*	to go out

B verbs ending in *-iru*

Transitive		**Intransitive**	
kiru	to wear	*koriru*	to learn from
niru	to boil		bitter experience
oriru	to descend	*ikiru*	to live, be alive
kariru	to borrow	*akiru*	to lose interest in

Ten more B verbs are listed in the chart showing their conjugations.

The plain past tense of the B verbs is shown in this chart. It is always made by adding *-ta* to the basic stem.

The construction of the gerund of the B verbs has already been explained. These gerunds plus *iru* or *imasu* form the progressive present while the addition of *ita* or *imashita* forms the progressive past.

Cultural sidelights:

*** Thanks for the other day. *Senjitsu wa dōmo (arigatō gozaimashita.)* The Japanese must be endowed with excellent memories for they unfailingly recall who did what for whom at the last meeting. Whether the favor was small or large, whether it was yesterday or a month ago, they never forget to say thanks. Adopting this custom will facilitate your social progress in Japan.

***We have met several terms for relatives: aunt, uncle, older sister, younger brother, and so forth. (In Japanese, you must specify older or younger sister and older or younger brother.) In addition to their obvious use, these are used in other ways not common in English. Children usually call the parents of their friends *ojisan* or *obasan,* not Mr. or Mrs. So-and-so. If they are obviously older than the customer, shopkeepers are often so addressed as well. Waitresses are sometimes called *oneisan,* although this is not to be encouraged. You should call your spouse's mother or father *okāsan* or *otōsan.* But draw the line at teachers and doctors. They should be called *sensei,* always.

***As explained in the vocabulary, *asobu* is a verb meaning to be idle or to be having a good time. A prominent meaning given in the dictionary is "to play," so we sometimes hear older, dignified gentlemen say something like, "I spent the afternoon playing in the park." To put this in its proper light, remember that the Japanese divide the day into time for sleep, time for work, and time for doing other things not of an essential nature, including doing nothing. It is this last category that is meant by the verb *asobu.*

***We have discussed the desiderative *-tai* that is added to the stem of a verb. *-tai* may be used about oneself and the immediate members of his family but if you are speaking to a superior, you should not say, *Unagi ga tabetai desu ka.* (Do you wish to eat eel?) Rather, you should say, *Unagi wa ikaga desu ka* (How about some eel?) or just go ahead and serve the eel. It embarrasses the Japanese to have to be specific about their desires. In Japan, a person's wishes are largely regarded as a private matter, and it is better not to ask about them directly.

The same cautions apply to the adjective *hoshii.* For instance, rather than ask a guest, *Doa wo shimete hoshii desu ka* (Do you want me to close the door?), it would be preferable to ask for instructions, *Doa wo shimemashō ka.* Shall I close the door?

Study recommendations:

At first, some students tend to hesitate and even to mumble when speaking their rudimentary *Nihongo.* It is far better, however, to speak clearly and with confidence, even though you may be making mistakes.

When practicing alone, you should also utter your words and sentences in a strong voice. Never mind that other occupants of the same dwelling may mock you. A clear, ringing voice will enhance your confidence, something most of us need in the early stages of the fray.

Lesson Eight

A.) Pronouns

B.) Time

Useful Everyday Expressions

Itadakimasu.	I accept (it) with respect and gratitude. Used when you accept anything from someone. Often prefaced by *enryo-naku* (without reserve). Always used just before eating or drinking as someone's guest.
Nanji desu ka.	What time is it?
Kyō wa ii o-tenki desu, ne.	
	It's a nice day, isn't it?
Shitsurei shimasu.	I am about to be rude. More politely, *Shitsurei itashimasu.* Used when approaching a stranger with a request or when about to enter another's home or a superior's office. And even when about to sit down and make yourself comfortable in another's quarters. *Senjitsu wa shitsurei shimashita* is "I was rude the other day" (even if you were not in the least rude). One of the assassins of a pre-war prime minister said *Shitsurei shimashita* to the dying politician's wife as he was fleeing from their residence. Another one of those ritualistic phrases whose continual repetition will take the speaker far in Japan.
Kutabare.	Drop dead.

Vocabulary

Because of the large number of new words and phrases that will be introduced under *How to Use* in this lesson, the vocabulary section is omitted.

Pattern Sentences

(Bunkei)

1. *Mikka ni kite kudasai.* Please come on the third (of the month).
2. *Mikka (-kan) uchi ni tomatte hoshii.* I want you to stay in my home for three days.
3. *Kaeri no fune wa futatsuki kakarimasu.* The return ship takes two months. Note this usage of the stem of the verb *kaeru*, to return, and the possessive *no.* Here the verb stem functions as a noun.
4. *Mō goji-han desu ka.* Is it already five-thirty?
5. *(Watakushi wa) sono dame na jogakusei wo ichijikan-han matte imashita.* I was waiting an hour and a half for that no-good coed.
6. *Ippun wa rokujū-byō desu.* There are sixty seconds in a minute.
7. *Kyō wa nanyō-bi desu ka.* What day of the week is today?
8. *Kono keshikaran shukudai wa hannichi kakatta.* This damnable homework took (me) half a day.
9. *Mai-nichiyō-bi kyōkai ni itte nemurimasu.* Every Sunday I go to church and sleep.
10. *Ano kata-gata wa han-jikan de Kōbe ni hashirimashita.* They ran to Kobe in half an hour.
11. *Ichinichi wa nijūgoji-kan desu ka. Chigaimasu.* Is one day twenty-five hours? No, it is not.
12. *Konna jikan ni warui ga...* My apologies (for bothering you at) such an hour. (Lit., Such a time—at—bad—but...)
13. *Kono oishii uni wa donata mo tabemasen ka.* Won't anyone eat this delicious sea urchin?
14. *Sono omoshiroku-nai shōsetsu wa nisen-en? Tonde mo nai!* Two thousand yen for that dull novel? Ridiculous!
15. *Kanai wa kekkon shite iru ga watakushi wa mada desu. Kekkon shite iru* means "is married," but I will let the student figure out the rest of this old joke.
16. *Honjitsu wa seireki no nannen, nangatsu, nannichi deshō ka.* By the Western calendar, what day, month, and year is today? (Whereas *desu* means is, am, or are, *deshō* carries the sense of future probability—"may be". Often, however, it is the same as *desu* but merely softens the directness of the question.)
17. *Bikkuri shimashita yo. Kare no kanojo wa baishumfu desu tte.* How surprised I was! They say his girlfriend is a woman of the streets. (Lit., His 'her'—as for—spring-selling woman—is—they say. *Tte* is a short way of saying *to iu.*)

How to Use

Pronouns

I have read that there are more than a hundred ways to say 'I' in Japanese as well as a plethora of words for 'you.' Although I cannot confirm that, I suspect that the estimate is factual, if it includes the archaic pronouns.

At the same time, Japanese have a pronounced tendency to avoid the use of pronouns, especially the personal ones. A brief dialog (in Japanese) like the following would not be considered odd:

"(I) think (it) will become cold tonight."

"(I) agree."

"Are (you) going out?"

"(I) will go out."

"Well then, (you) had better wear an overcoat."

"(I) will. Will Mother go out, too?" *

"No, (I) will not go out. (It) is too cold."

*The speaker is talking to his mother.

The words in parentheses are understood but not expressed. Result? No pronouns.

Often the polite or plain form of the verb and the honorific prefix do the work of the pronoun. (More about this lesser reliance on pronouns under Cultural Sidelights in this lesson.)

Foreign students use the Japanese equivalents of 'I' and 'you' far too often in their speech because they are thinking in (English) and interpreting their thoughts literally, word for word. That is to say, they are not relying enough on the pattern sentence method recommended herein.

Even so, such pronouns cannot be avoided entirely. Indeed, they are at times essential to clarity and so must be learned. We have met some of these in earlier lessons.

	Singular	**Plural**
I	*watashi* or *watakushi*	*watashi-tachi, watakushi-tachi*
you	*anata* (standard)	*anata-tachi, anata-gata*
	kimi (masculine, among close friends)	*kimi-tachi*
	omae (said to inferiors)	*omae-tachi*
he, she	*kono hito* (standard)	*kono hito-tachi* (they)
	sono hito (standard)	*sono hito-tachi* (they)
	ano hito (standard)	*ano hito-tachi* (they)
he	*kare* (refer to Cultural Sidelights)	*kare-tachi* (they) *kare-ra* (they)
she	*kanojo* (refer to Cultural Sidelights)	*kanojo-tachi* (they)
he, she	*ano ko* (that child)*	*ano ko-tachi,* etc. (they)

*(also, *kono ko, sono ko*)

Japanese pronouns have no case. Thus, *watashi* can be either I or me.

Possessive pronouns are readily constructed by the addition of *no. Watashi no biiru wo sawaru na!* means, Hands off my beer! The negative imperative (do not...) of any verb is formed by saying *na* after the verb's dictionary form. This is informal and rather rough.

Iku na.	Don't go.
Naku na.	Don't cry.
Hanasu na.	Don't speak.

In the above, you will see *kono hito, sono hito,* and *ano hito* given as he or she. In an earlier lesson, the student was told, in the part about the *ko, so, a,* and *do* words, that *kono* (as well as *kore,* etc.) refers to something that is near to hand, *sono* means something near the listener, and *ano* describes something farther away from both the speaker and the listener. This is true of inanimate objects, but in the case of animate objects, the distinction between *sono* and *ano* depends not on distance of separation but on whether the listener knows the animate object being mentioned. *Ano hito,* then, would be a person the listener knows, while *sono hito* would be someone he may not.

Interrogative Pronoun	Meaning	Add *ka*	Meaning
dore	which	*dore ka*	one of
nani	what	*nani ka*	something
doko	where	*doko ka*	somewhere
dare	who	*dare ka*	some one
ikutsu	how many	*ikutsu ka*	a few
itsu	when	*itsu ka*	some time or other
ikura	how much	*ikura ka*	a little or a certain amount
donata	who (politer than *dare*)	*donata ka*	someone
dochira	which way, which	*dochira ka*	either, whichever
dotchi	which way, which	*dotchi ka*	either, whichever
dō	how	*dō ka*	somehow or the other

The lesson on polite and plain words and phrases will have more to say about other pronouns, but the above will provide for most of your needs for the nonce.

The plural form *-gata* is somewhat more respectful than *-tachi*.

The student should refer again to the "*ko, so, a,* and *do* word" chart in Lesson Three to find the basic demonstrative, interrogative, and directional pronouns. In the vocabulary lists are given other pronouns: *nani* (what), *ikutsu* (how many), and *itsu* (when). In *nani,* the final *i* is omitted *(nan)* before any word that starts with *d, n,* or *t.* Thus, *Sore wa nan desu ka* (What is that?)

Add mo	Meaning	Add demo	Meaning
dore mo	none	*dore de mo*	any one*at all
nani mo	nothing	*nan de mo*	anything at all
doko mo	nowhere	*doko de mo*	anywhere
dare mo	no one	*dare de mo*	any one
ikutsu mo	a very few	*ikutsu de mo*	any number
itsu mo	always	*itsu de mo*	at any time
ikura mo	any amount or number. (with negative, not many or not much)	*ikura de mo*	any amount
donata mo	no one	*donata de mo*	any one
dochira mo	both, neither	*dochira de mo*	either
dotchi mo	both, neither	*dotchi de mo*	either
dō mo	how, very much, really	*dō de mo*	any way, anyhow, as one pleases

*refers to objects, not persons

Bear in mind that when you use an interrogative pronoun as the sentence's subject, it should always be followed by *ga* and not *wa*. *Dare ga sonna baka na koto wo itta ka.* (Who said such a stupid thing?)

Concerning the possible omission of the subject of a sentence (whether it be a pronoun or not), a rule to remember is: When asked a question about someone or something that is the subject of the question sentence, it is better not to repeat that subject in your answer.

Ano sensei wa gozen jūji ni miemasu ka shira.

I wonder if that teacher will appear at ten o'clock in the morning?

Mieru deshō.

(He or she) will probably appear.

A simple way to increase your vocabulary substantially is by using *ka, mo,* or *de mo* after the interrogative pronouns:

About the *'de mo'* given above: It actually has three meanings, one of them being 'even' or 'any' as in *Ano otonashisō na buchō de mo uwaki wo shimasu.* Even that meek section chief is a philanderer.

In a second sense, *de mo* means "... or something." For instance, *Taikutsu nara shimbun de mo yonde kudasai.* If you are bored, please read a newspaper or something.

The third usage of *de mo* is 'too'—as shown in the following example: *Kankoku-go de mo dekimasu.* I can handle Korean, too.

Japanese has no relative pronouns. In English, we use relative pronouns in sentences like the "Bird that cannot fly" and the "Athlete who cannot run" and "The whip which the teacher often uses." In Japanese, these become:

Tobenai kotori	Lit., Cannot—fly—bird
Hashirenai undōka	Lit., Cannot—run—athlete
Sensei ga yoku tsukau muchi	Lit., Teacher—as for—often—use whip.

The potential voice of verbs—e.g., *tobenai, hashirenai*—will be explained in due course. Be patient.

Time

First, an attempt should be made to explain the two main words meaning time: *toki* and *jikan.*

Generally (but not always), *toki* means a specific point in time, such as 3:43 p.m. today, and *jikan* means a period of time, such as the 'one hour' in "I waited one hour for her". The *kanji* for *toki* is 時 and those for *jikan* are 時間, so you can see that the Chinese reading of *toki*, which is *ji*, is the first of the two *kanji* for *jikan*, while the second is *kan* (or *aida*) for duration.

Sometimes, however, these two words invade each other's territory, as in these examples:

tadashii jikan	the correct time
jikan made ni tsuku	to arrive in time
Toki ga tatsu.	Time passes. (This *tatsu* is not the one that means to stand.)
toki ga aru	to have time
toki wo kasegu	to buy time (*kasegu* means to earn)
Toki wa kane nari.	Time is money.

Despite these and other exceptions, we should, for the present, live with the explanation above.

The word for minute is *fun* and that for hour is *ji,* although these are not used alone. Both are used with the Chinese numbers we have already studied. *Ichi* and *fun* become *ippun*—one minute, *ni* and *fun* become *nifun*—two minutes, and so forth.

ippun	1 minute
nifun	2 minutes
sampun	3 minutes
yompun	4 minutes
gofun	5 minutes
roppun	6 minutes
nanafun (or *shichifun*)	7 minutes
hachifun (or *happun*)	8 minutes
kyūfun	9 minutes
jippun	10 minutes
jūippun	11 minutes
jūnifun	12 minutes
nijippun	20 minutes

and so on.

The hours are:

ichiji	1 o'clock
niji	2 o'clock
sanji	3 o'clock
yoji (not *yonji*)	4 o'clock
goji	5 o'clock
rokuji	6 o'clock
shichiji	7 o'clock
hachiji	8 o'clock
kuji	9 o'clock
jūji	10 o'clock
jūichiji	11 o'clock
jūniji	12 o'clock

Add *-kan* to, say, *niji* (two o'clock) and we have *niji-kan* or two hours. But *niji* alone must always mean two o'clock. *Nifun-kan* is the period of time 'two minutes' (120 seconds), but the *nifun* in *niji nifun sugi* (two minutes past two o'clock) is also a period of time.

-goro is used for 'about' with a specific time, as in *shichiji goro* (about seven o'clock). For a period of time, however, *-goro* is not used. "It took about ten hours" is said as *Jūji-kan kurai kakarimashita,* with *kurai* or (*gurai* with the phonetic change) being the 'about' in this instance. Later, you will learn other ways to express the same thought.

Ima is the most common word for 'now,' but sometimes the demonstrative pronoun *kore* (this) is used instead. *Kore kara* equals 'from now on,' *sore kara* is 'after that' in either the future or past, but *are kara* ('after that') must have reference only to a past time.

A *byō* is one second. Seconds are counted:

ichibyō	1 second
nibyō	2 seconds
sambyō	3 seconds
yombyō	4 seconds
gobyō	5 seconds
rokubyō	6 seconds
nanabyō	7 seconds
hachibyō	8 seconds

and so on.

Midnight and twelve noon are expressed as *reiji* or the zero hour. Noon is also *shōgo*. *Reiji sampun sugi* is three minutes after noon or three minutes after midnight.

To say the exact time, one reverses the order from English. Ten minutes past eight o'clock is *hachiji jippun sugi* (eight o'clock—ten minutes—after). *Sugi,* meaning 'after,' is from the verb *sugiru*—to exceed, to pass—but it is often omitted, especially as the number of minutes increases. For 'before,' substitute *mae* for *sugi,* although one can say *gofun de rokuji,* to mean five until six o'clock, or *jūnifun de gozen no sanji* to mean twelve minutes before three a.m.

Thirteen minutes past two o'clock	*Niji jūsanpun (sugi)*
Nine minutes before eight o'clock	*Hachiji kyūfun mae*

Six-thirty can be said as *rokuji sanjippun (sugi)* or *rokuji-han,* the *-han* being the word for half.

Half past two	*Niji-han*
Five-thirty	*Goji sanjippun*

The particle *ni* after any of these phrases means 'at'.

Reiji ni ikimasu. (I) will go at midnight (or noon).
Goji-han ni tabemashō. Let's eat at five-thirty.

To distinguish between a.m. and p.m., use *gozen* for the former and *gogo* for the latter.

Gozen jūichiji sampun sugi desu. It is three minutes past eleven a. m.
Mō gogo yoji gofun desu ka. Is it already five minutes after four in the afternoon?

Another word for morning, *asa,* may be said instead of *gozen,* but it is usually followed by *no.*

Asa no sanji ni okimasu. I will get up at three in the morning.

For the afternoon hours, there is no substitute for *gogo,* but at night you can say, for example, *yoru no kuji* (nine in the evening) instead of *gogo no kuji.* While *gogo no kuji* is technically correct, *yoru no kuji* is more common.

The simplicity of the days of the week, at least, warms the heart. To the already-mastered (I trust) Chinese numerals, you simply add *-gatsu.* That and nothing more. No phonetic or orthographic changes:

ichi-gatsu	January	*shichi-gatsu*	July
ni-gatsu	February	*hachi-gatsu*	August
san-gatsu	March	*kugatsu*	September
shi-gatsu	April	*jūgatsu*	October
(never *yon-gatsu)*		*jūichi-gatsu*	November
go-gatsu	May	*jūni-gatsu*	December
roku-gatsu	June		

Sometimes *shō-gatsu* is used for January, but if you prefix the honorific *o (o-shō-gatsu),* the meaning changes to the New Year's holidays, which are the first three days of January.

Note that April, July, and September are always *shi-gatsu, shichi-gatsu,* and *ku-gatsu*—never *yon-gatsu, nana-gatsu,* and *kyū-gatsu.*

Other references to months are:

nangatsu	which month
nankagetsu-kan	how many months
sengetsu	last month
raigetsu	next month
sen-sengetsu	month before last
rai-raigetsu	month after next
kongetsu	this month
gokagetsu mae	five months ago
jikkagetsu mae	ten months ago

The *kanji* for month is 月, which has the additional meaning of moon. This character may be pronounced *tsuki, -gatsu,* or *-getsu.* As periods of time, months are counted with both the Chinese and the Japanese numerals:

Chinese		Japanese
ikkagetsu	one month	*hitotsuki*
nikagetsu	two months	*futatsuki*
sankagetsu	three months	*mitsuki*
shi(yon)kagetsu	four months	*yotsuki*
gokagetsu	five months	*itsutsuki**
rokkagetsu	six months	*mutsuki**
shichi(nana)kagetsu	seven months	*nanatsuki**
hachikagetsu	eight months	*yatsuki**
kukagetsu	nine months	*kokonotsuki**
jikkagetsu	ten months	*totsuki*
jūikkagetsu	eleven months	
jūnikagetsu	twelve months	

* Seldom used

The *ka* that follows the Chinese numerals above is written ヶ and is a numerator for small objects that can be handled. (More about this later).

Years are counted only with the Chinese numerals:

ichinen	one year	*rokunen*	six years
ninen	two years	*shichinen*	
sannen	three years	*(nananen)*	seven years
yonen	four years	*hachinen*	eight years
gonen	five years	*kyūnen*	nine years
		jūnen	ten years

"Ten years ago" may be expressed as *jūnen mae (ni)* or *jūnen-kan mae (ni).* That is, in the case of both months and years, *-kan* (which means duration) may be added or omitted. Because the meaning does not change, most opt to omit the *-kan* nowadays.

Insertion of the same *ka*—as in the *ikkagetsu, nikagetsu,* et al above—in *ichinen* and *sannen-kan* gives us *ikkanen, sankanen-kan,* and so forth, which are also used.

Nihongo wo oboeru ni wa jūnen (ga) kakarimashita is the same as *Nihongo wo oboeru ni wa junen-kan kakarimashita.* It took 10 years to learn Japanese. *Uchi no obasan wa nikagetsu buta-bako ni imashita* equals *Uchi no obasan wa nikagetsu-kan buta-bako ni imashita.* (*Buta-bako* or 'pig-box' is slang for jail.) A third option is, *Uchi no obasan wa futatsuki (or futatsuki-kan) buta-bako ni imashita.* All three examples mean, My aunt was in jail for two months.

Although the suffixing of *-kan* is optional with days, months, and years, it is required with seconds, minutes, and hours.

Six years may be *rokunen* or *rokunen-kan.*
Two days may be *futsuka* or *futsuka-kan.*
Seven months may be *nanatsuki* or *nanatsuki-kan.*
But nine seconds must be *kyūbyō-kan.*
Five hours must be *goji-kan.*
Four minutes must be *yompun-kan.*
(This does not apply to the minutes after an hour.
Four minutes after five o'clock is *Goji yompun sugi.*)

The ordinal sense of years, months, and days (see the following) is expressed by the suffix *-me.*

yonen-me	the fourth year
rokkagetsu-me	the sixth month
yōka-me	the eighth day (See below also.)

'The first' is translated as *hajime no.* (*Hajime* is the stem of the transitive verb *hajimeru,* to begin.)

hajime no gonen-kan	the first five years
hajime no totsuki	the first ten months

The days of the month are:

tsuitachi or		*yokka*	4th
ichijitsu	1st (day)	*itsuka*	5th
futsuka	2nd	*muika*	6th
mikka	3rd	*nanoka (nanuka)*	7th

yōka	8th	*hatsuka*	20th
kokonoka	9th	*nijūichi-nichi*	21st
tōka	10th	*nijūni-nichi*	22nd
jūichi-nichi	11th	*nijūsan-nichi*	23rd
jūni-nichi	12th	*nijūyokka*	24th
jūsan-nichi	13th	*nijūgo-nichi*	25th
jūyokka	14th	*nijūroku-nichi*	26th
jūgo-nichi	15th	*nijūshichi-nichi*	27th
jūroku-nichi	16th	*nijūhachi-nichi*	28th
jūshichi-nichi	17th	*nijūku-nichi*	29th
jūhachi-nichi	18th	*sanjū-nichi*	30th
jūku-nichi	19th	*sanjūichi-nichi*	31st

There are some irregularities in the above, so a close look is advised.

Although written with the same *kanji* (一日) as *tsuitachi* or *ichijitsu* (1st day), *ichinichi* means 'one day'. From the 2nd through the 31st day, the Japanese equivalents can mean either number of days or such-and-such a day of the month. If the reference is to the number of days, then *-kan* may be added or left off.

Misoka means the final day of any month, while *ō-misoka* (*ō* is a Chinese reading of the character for large, *ōkii*) refers to the last day of any year. *Ganjitsu* means the first day of any year.

Nannichi desu ka means What day is it? or How many days? while *Nannichi-kan desu ka* means only How many days?

The days of the week are as follows:

getsuyō (-bi)	Monday
kayō (-bi)	Tuesday
suiyō (-bi)	Wednesday
mokuyō (-bi)	Thursday
kinyō (-bi)	Friday
doyō (-bi)	Saturday
nichiyō (-bi)	Sunday

Adding the suffix *-bi* (for day) is standard practice, although it may be dropped and still be understood. When giving a series of days or of alternate days, only the first character is often used. If asked, On what days of the week do you have Japanese class? you could answer, *Getsu, sui, kin*—for Monday, Wednesday, and Friday.

As you progress in your *kanji* studies, you will find that the first *kanji* in the days of the week mean moon, fire, water, tree, metal, earth, and sun successively.

In our Periods of Time chart in Lesson Six, we showed how *mai* was used to mean 'every,' as in every day, every year, etc. *Mai* can also be applied to days of the week, as in *mai-mokuyō-bi* for every Thursday, and so forth.

By adding *goto ni* to a word for a period of time, we also introduce the meaning of 'every.' *Jūnen goto ni* is every ten years; *mikka goto ni* is every three days; *hachiji-kan goto ni* is every eight hours.

'Every' can also be expressed by *oki* or *oki ni. Gobyō oki ni* is every five seconds; *ichiman-nen oki* is every ten thousand years.

Mae is used for 'ago.' *Yonshū-kan mae* is four weeks ago; *sankagetsu-kan-han mae ni* is three and a half months ago.

Kisetsu is the word for season, and the four seasons are expressed as *shiki* (which happens to be the name of more than a few Japanese restaurants).

haru	spring
natsu	summer
aki	autumn
fuyu	winter

In English, uncertainty about periods of time is seen in such phrases as two or three days, eight or nine months, and twenty or thirty years. A conjunction, as you see, always plays a role, but in Japanese it is usually omitted. *Ni-sannichi* is two or three days, and *nijūshi-go* is twenty-four or twenty-five.

In Japan, days of the week and months of the year correspond to their Western equivalents, but there are two ways of giving the year. In the Japanese way of counting calendar years, an era begins with the ascension of a new emperor to the throne and ends with his passing. Thus, 1988, for instance, was *Shōwa rokujūsan-nen* or the 63rd year of Showa. Each *nengō* or era name is different, *Shōwa* meaning brilliant harmony and *Meiji* expressing Enlightened Rule. The full date is given in reverse order, November 23, 1988 becoming *Shōwa rokujūsan-nen jūichigatsu nijū-san-nichi.* The Western calendar year is also used, 1988 being *issen kyūhyaku hachijūhachi-nen.*

To ask a person's age, say,
Toshi wa o-ikutsu desu ka.   (Lit., How many years have you?)
or
Nan-sai desu ka.

An adult will answer with a Chinese numeral and the suffix *-sai.* Thus, *nijūroku-sai* is 26 years old. Children ten or under often use only the Japanese numeral, *Yattsu desu* being, I am eight years old and *Itsutsu da yo* meaning, I'm five!

You should also review the Periods of Time chart in Lesson Six at this stage.

Cultural sidelights:

  *** In an earlier lesson, we had the sentence, "Let me introduce my wife," in which *tsuma* was used for 'my wife.' In this lesson, we find another word for 'my wife'—*kanai.* Both are humble words used in reference to one's own wife, who may also use them about herself.

Often, however, the Japanese avoid all such words. A husband may neglect to introduce his wife at all or merely wave a casual hand in her direction while mumbling indistinct words. Even the wife may avoid identifying herself clearly. When she telephones her husband's favorite bar *(yukitsuke no bā)*—which she would seldom dare do—she might ask, *Morimoto wa imasu ka.* Her act of *yobisute,* e.g., saying the family name without a title, identifies her as a member of one of Morimoto's households, but we have no way of knowing if she is the mother or daughter or a maiden aunt or a mistress.

In any event, *tsuma* is rather formal, though humble. More informal expressions are *nyōbō* and *uchi no yatsu.*

*** Pronouns are largely avoided in Japanese for two principal reasons. One is that, as noted earlier, Westerners look upon man as the center of the sentient universe while Orientals tend more to the view that man is merely a pebble on the beach—in a cosmos with millions of beaches. The second—and more practical—reason is that pronouns reflect how the speaker ranks the person spoken to or about. If I say *kisama* (an insulting pronoun for 'you') in speaking to someone, he will be terribly hurt—or, worse, he may hurt me terribly. Or I may go to the opposite extreme and, while doing a *kōtō* bow (in which the forehead touches the floor), call him *"tono-sama"* (mighty lord). And there are several gradations in between, most of them also being fraught with risks. Better, the Japanese seem to think, to avoid pronouns whenever one can and let the plain and polite verb forms and other devices do their work for them.

*** *Kare* and *kanojo* have been given as the pronouns for he and she (or him and her). Both of these pronouns came into fairly common use only after Japan's exposure to Western languages in the early Meiji era and the realization that the native pronouns, such as they were, provided no easy way to identify the sex of the person being spoken about. Making a clear gender distinction did not seem to be a matter of much importance, anyway. Even today, proper speakers of Japanese look askance at those two pronouns as being rather impolite. I recall one memorable night in the 1950's when my Japanese landlord (he was the land owner; I had built the house) came in and kept referring to my mistress as *"kanojo."* Well, I didn't care for him to begin with. He was a haughty throw-back to the arrogant landlords of feudal times. Finally, he called her *"kanojo"* once too often, so I evicted him bodily. In our Omori neighborhood (where he owned most of the land), this defenestration incident became the *cause celebre* of the year.

Anyway, *kare* and *kanojo* should be limited in use to those with whom one is on close terms, never outsiders to whom one should show respect.

It is not uncommon for wives to refer to their husbands as *kare,* and *kanojo* carries the colloquial meaning of girlfriend. The latter can result in such grammatical oddities as *kare no kanojo* (his her), as demonstrated in the *bunkei.*

*** The last pattern sentence above contained the word *baishumpu,* which is written with the three *kanji* for sell—spring—woman. It means prostitute and is a prime example of Japanese delicacy in dealing with the earthy and indecorous.

*** Take care to distinguish between the use of *shitsurei shimasu* (Useful Everyday Expressions above) and *shitsurei desu ga...* The former is said when you are about to take leave of someone (as well as in the instances given earlier), but the latter is used before asking a delicate question. During a tete-a-tete with a friend, you might be on the point of asking a personal question, but if you prefaced it with the former in lieu of the latter, he might stand up and bid you God speed, thinking you had announced your intention of departing.

*** The depth of the obeisance must depend on circumstances, but it is always better to bow when using such apologetic expressions as *shitsurei shimasu, shitsurei desu ga..., ayamarimasu, o-wabi shimasu, o-yurushi kudasai,* et al.

The one exception might be when you say *Gomen nasai,* which is somewhat childish and feminine in tone. The apology implied in these two words is quite casual and really does not need to be fortified by a bending of the back or a knuckling of the forelock.

Lesson Nine

A.) Irregular verbs

B.) Adverbs

C.) *-nagara* (while, although)

D.) *Tsumori* (intention)

E.) *Kara, node,* and *naze ka to iu to* (because)

Useful Everyday Expressions

Ikemasen yo.   Don't do (it)., (Lit., It cannot go.)

Tadaima   I'm home. (Lit., just now.) Always said when one returns home. Short for *Tadaima kaerimashita* (I've just now returned.)

Sō ka mo shiremasen.

It may be so. Often used in place of *Sō desu* when one does not wish to be too direct or straight-forward.

Osoku narimashite....

Lit., Becoming lately... Actually means I'm sorry for being late. Another of those seemingly incomplete thoughts that the Japanese love.

Ii o-sumai desu, ne.   What a nice house you have. You may never be shown through the interior of a Japanese home, but if you ever are, you may feel charitably disposed to praise the dwelling with such words as these.

O-jōzu desu ne.   How skillful you are! We are told by some authorities that it is better not to express such praise directly to anyone to whom you must use respectful language. The idea is that it is presumptuous to openly evaluate the skill of a superior. However, you will find that this does not in the least restrain most Japanese from saying those very words to any foreigner whose Japanese vocabulary exceeds seven or possibly eight words. My advice? The devil take such picayunish protocol.

(Kōhī) wo dōzo...

Or, *Biiru wo dōzo... O-cha wo dōzo...* Another of those incomplete sentences like *Osoku narimashite...* above. Somehow it doesn't sound quite right to finish the thought and say, *Kōhī wo dōzo nonde kudasai.* (Please drink the coffee.)

Vocabulary

Fukushi wo takusan shōkai shimasu node tango no tokoro wo mata habukimasu. (Because I will introduce many adverbs, I will again omit the vocabulary section.)

Pattern Sentences
(Bunkei)

1. *Chotto no aida hyaku-en bakari kashite kudasai.* Please lend me about ¥100 for a little while.
2. *Tokidoki kaze ga hyūhyū fukimasu.* Sometimes the wind blows with a whistling sound.
3. *Tonari no neko wa itsumo uchi no niwa ni imasu.* The neighbor's cat is always in our garden.
4. *Hakkiri hatsuon shite kudasai.* Please pronounce clearly.
5. *Uchi no niwa-shi ga wani ni kuwareta kara mō hitori sagashite imasu.* Because our gardener was eaten by alligators, I am searching for another (gardener).
6. *Mō ichido yari-nasai.* Do it again.
7. *Mazu ayamareba ii desu.* First, you should apologize.
8. *Mō takusan desu.* That is already enough.
9. *Itsu ikimasu ka.* When are you going? *Mō itte kimashita.* I have already gone and come back.
10. *Boku wa saikin o-naka ga dete kimashita.* Lately my stomach has begun to stick out. (In a few instances the honorific *o* can be used about yourself. Thus, *o-naka* (honorable middle) can mean your own stomach. If you said just *naka,* no one would take that word— without the prefix *o*—to mean stomach.)
11. *Kyō dekakeru tsumori wa arimasen.* I do not intend to go out today.
12. *Kesshite uso wa tsukimasen.* I never lie.
    The adverb *kesshite* (never) is used to describe a person's attitude or will, not forces not under human control. You should not use it, for instance, to say, It never rains in the Sahara.
13. *Hontō ni oishiku miemasu.* It looks simply delicious, (*Mieru* means 'to be seen as' as well as 'to be visible' and 'to be able to see'.)

How to Use

Irregular Verbs

There are only two fully conjugated irregular verbs, and both are often used. In fact, one of them (*suru,* to do) is probably used more often than any other verb, aside from the copulas *desu* and *(de) arimasu.* And there are a few others only slightly irregular.

First, let's see how the two main ones are conjugated. Beside them we will then conjugate *iku* or *yuku* (to go), which is one of the slightly irregular verbs.

Dictionary Form	*kuru* (come)	*suru* (do, etc.)	*iku* or *yuku** (go)
Basic Stem	*ki-*	*shi-*	*iki-*
Negative Stem	*ko-*	*shi-*	*ika-*
Plain Imperative	*koi*	*shiro, seyo*	*ike*
Conditional Stem	*kure (ba)*	*shi (tara), sure (ba)*	*ike (ba), ittara*
Suggestive or Conditional	*koyō*	*shiyō*	*ikō*
Gerund	*kite*	*shite*	*itte*
Plain Past Tense	*kita*	*shita*	*itta*
Basic Stem with *-masu*	*kimasu*	*shimasu*	*ikimasu*
Polite Past Tense	*kimashita*	*shimashita*	*ikimashita*

* *Yuku* is used more west of Nagoya.

Suru's basic meaning is 'to do,' but it has others you should remember:

To cost, as in *Kono bōshi wa issen-en suru.*
(This hat costs one thousand yen.)

To have, as in *Zutsū ga suru.*
  (To have a headache)
To run, as in *Shōbai wo suru.*   (To run a business)
To serve or act as, as in *Untenshu wo suru*
  (To work as a driver)
To make of, as in *Musuko wo bengoshi ni suru*
  (To make a lawyer of one's son)
To act, behave, as in *Nombiri suru* (To act leisurely)
To hear, as in *Koe ga suru* (to hear a voice)

But, to repeat, the basic meaning is 'to do,' as in *Shigoto wo suru* (To do one's work).

Suru can be given in English as 'to make' as well as 'to do.'

Tabi wo suru	to make a trip
Machigai wo suru	to make a mistake
O-jigi wo suru	to make a bow

Obviously, in the above three examples as well as in many others, you could use a single English verb to express the same meaning, e.g. to travel, to err, and to bow.

When asked if you will give your firm promise *(Kataku yakusoku suru ka),* your answer, if affirmative, could be just *Suru* (I will) or *Yakusoku suru* (I will promise.)

The polite form of *suru* is *shimasu* (*suru's* negative is *shinai* or, politely, *shimasen*), which you should be using much more than *suru* at this stage in your studies.

If we take the basic stem of *suru,* which is *shi-,* we can add certain other verbs, such as *naosu* (to correct) and *ageru* (to lift, raise, give), and thereby modify the meaning, as in these examples:

shi-naosu	to repeat, to do again
shi-ageru	to complete

Or we can add certain pure adjectives, like *nikui* and *katai*. Both mean 'difficult' and are written with the same *kanji* (難).

shi-nikui	hard to do
shi-gatai	hard to do (the *k* changes phonetically to *g*)

A noun followed by *suru* may be called a noun-verb. The noun may be a single-*kanji* noun (like *tabi* above) or a compound noun made up of two or more *kanji*. There are a vast number of these noun-verbs, so many and varied that it may seem that the Japanese attach *suru* to any noun promiscuously, but this would be an exaggeration.

The nouns in these "noun-verbs" are often of Chinese origin, e.g., they are compounded of two *kanji* as with *benkyō* (勉強) for study, *kekkon* (結婚) for marriage, *kanshin* (感心) for admiration, and *ryokō* (旅行) for travel. Although written separately, these Chinese compound nouns plus *suru* approach the unity of a single verb and so usually do not require the intervening accusative marker *wo*.

benkyō suru	to study
kekkon suru	to marry
kanshin suru	to admire
ryokō suru	to travel

They may even attach *suru* to imported English nouns like:

kyanseru suru	to cancel
sukī suru	to ski
erā suru	to commit an error, usually in baseball

Using *suru* with such imported words does not follow an orderly pattern but seems to be based more on whimsy and the urge to display a degree of international savoir-faire.

By taking the basic stem of a verb and adding *wa shinai* or *wa shimasen*, you will have formed a negative that is quite emphatic.

Tobi wa shimasen.	I will not fly.
Iki wa shimasen.	I will not go.
Ijime wa shimasen.	I will not abuse.

If you drop the final *i* in a Class A adjective, replace the *i* with *ku,* and follow that with *suru,* you will have the meaning of "to make..."

nagaku suru	to make long
oishiku suru	to make delicious

Or follow a Class B adjective with *ni suru* for the same effect.

kirei ni suru	to make pretty
anzen ni suru	to make safe

-ni shitai (the desiderative form of *suru*) can be used to express your wish that something will come about.

Chichi ga genki ni naru yō ni shitai mono desu.
  I hope father will regain his health.
Raishū ryokō suru kara o-tenki ni shitai mono desu.
  Because I will travel next week, I hope the weather will be good. (*O-tenki* or 'honorable' weather is always taken to mean 'good' weather. How could anything considered honorable ever disappoint us?)

Other than its irregular conjugation, there is nothing remarkable about the second irregular verb *kuru,* to come. Just remember to pronounce the two *u* sounds as short vowels. If you elongate the second *u,* you will have uttered the verb *kuruu,* which means to go crazy. There's no need to rush things.

The polite verbs *kudasaru* (to give, to bestow), *nasaru* (to do), *irassharu* (to go, to come, and to be), *ossharu* (to speak, to say), and *gozaru* (to be—politer than *arimasu*) are irregular in that the final syllable *(ru)* is replaced by *(i)* when the polite ending *-masu* is added. This gives us *kudasaimasu, nasaimasu, irasshaimasu, osshaimasu,* and *gozaimasu.* Their imperatives are *kudasai, nasai, irasshai,* and *osshai.* (*Gozai* should be the imperative of *gozaru,* but such a word is not used.) As polite verbs, the first four must not be used about the speaker or his group.

Gozaru (gozaimasu) may, however, be used in any situation that advises polite speech, in place of *arimasu. (Kore wa uchi no gusoku de gozaimasu.* This is my dumb son.) If, for instance, a person asks you if you have a car *(Jidōsha ga gozaimasu ka),* you may answer, Yes, I have *(Gozaimasu),* even though the verb is about your car and not someone else's.

Dictionary form	Meaning	Basic stem	With -*masu*
gozaru	to be	*gozai-*	*gozaimasu*
irassharu	to go, come, be	*irasshai-*	*irasshaimasu*
kudasaru	to (deign to) give	*kudasai-*	*kudasaimasu*
nasaru	to do	*nasai-*	*nasaimasu*
ossharu	to say	*osshai-*	*osshaimasu*

Adverbs

There is a cornucopia of adverbs in Japanese, and they come in several varieties. First, let's list some of what we shall call the true adverbs:

chōdo	just	*hotondo*	almost
mattaku	entirely	*yaya*	somewhat
mochiron	of course	*sae**	even
jissai	actually	*taitei*	as a rule
datte	even	*oyoso*	about
mata	moreover	*saikin*	recently
yaku	about	*onajiku*	similarly
zuibun	very	*tabun*	probably
toriwake	especially	*motto*	more
kanarazu	surely	*iwayuru*	so-called
tōtō	at last	*taezu*	incessantly
ōkata	nearly	*mō*	already
yagate	soon	*zutto*	all along, throughout
taihen	very		
mazu	to begin with	*tonikaku*	anyhow

*kiri**	only	*tsumari*	after all
osoraku	perhaps	*tatta*	only
arayuru	all sorts of	*omowazu*	unintentionally
kekkyoku	in the end	*kanari*	tolerably, fairly
semete	at least	*bakari**	only, about

* used only *after* the word modified.

Often adverbs come as the first word in a sentence.

The so-called A adjectives, taken up in Lesson Four, that end in *i* become adverbs when that *i* ending is changed to *ku:*

Adjective		Adverb	
shitashii	intimate	*shitashiku*	intimately
oishii	delicious	*oishiku*	deliciously
tanoshii	happy	*tanoshiku*	happily

Lesson Four also gave us the two classes of B adjectives: those followed by *na* and those followed by *no*. Many (but by no means all) of the former can work as adverbs if the *na* is exchanged for *ni*:

Adjective		Adverb	
shinsetsu (na)	kind	*shinsetsu (ni)*	kindly
jōsu (na)	skillful	*jōzu (ni)*	skillfully
shōjiki (na)	honest	*shōjiki (ni)*	honestly

About the B adjectives followed by *no*: If the *no* is omitted, many of these act as true adverbs, such as *sukoshi, taigai, taitei, yohodo,* and *chotto*. Some B adjectives in this class, however, must be followed by *ni* to become adverbial:

Adjective		Adverb	
hontō	truthful	*hontō ni*	truthfully
wazuka	slight	*wazuka ni*	slightly
igai	unexpected	*igai ni*	unexpectedly
atarimae	obvious	*atarimae ni*	obviously
tokubetsu	special	*tokubetsu ni*	specially

Some nouns, when followed by *de,* act as adverbs:

Noun		Adverb	
maru	entirety	*maru de*	entirely

The gerunds of some verbs are treated as adverbs:

Verb		Adverb	
hajimeru	to begin	*hajimete*	for first time
ochitsuku	to be calm	*ochitsuite*	calmly
awateru	to be in a confused hurry	*awatete*	in a confused hurry
kawaru	to change	*kawatte*	instead
kasaneru	to stack up	*kasanete*	repeatedly
kiwameru	to carry to extremes	*kiwamete*	exceedingly

There are some adverbs used only with negative verbs:

Sappari wakarimasen.	I don't understand at all.
Sukoshi mo hoshiku nai.	I don't want any at all.
Ikkō ni tsukaremasen.	I'm not tired at all.
Chittomo kamaimasen.	It doesn't matter in the least.

One large group of adverbs is followed by *ni,* like the converted B adjectives above:

sono ue ni	besides	*tama ni*	occasionally
toku ni	especially	*tsune ni*	ordinarily
shizen ni	naturally	*shidai ni*	gradually
o-make ni	in the bargain	*saiwai ni*	fortunately
rinji ni	temporarily	*shiawase ni*	happily
tagai ni	mutually	*yōi ni*	easily
muri ni	unreasonably	*makoto ni*	truly
kari ni	temporarily	*hijō ni*	unusually
hen ni	strangely	*fushigi ni*	strangely
fuchūi ni	carelessly	*gehin ni*	vulgarly
tokku ni	already	*ōi ni*	largely

In the same group are other adverbs after which the *ni* may be retained or may be omitted.

chokusetsu (ni)	directly	*tsugi (ni)*	next
futsū (ni)	usually	*sugu (ni)*	at once
dandan (ni)	gradually		

Then too we have those adverbs that end in the syllable *ri*. You may say *to* after these adverbs for emphasis:

hakkiri (to)	clearly	*yukkuri (to)*	slowly
kitchiri (to)	precisely	*sukkari (to)*	entirely
kossori (to)	stealthily	*tappuri (to)*	abundantly
shikkari (to)	firmly	*bonyari (to)*	absent-mindedly

In some instances, the *to* following certain adverbs has become such an integral part of them that the two parts are now inseparable:

kitto	surely	*chanto*	correctly
jitto	steadfastly	*yatto*	at length
sotto	softly	*hyotto*	possibly

There is yet another kind of adverb—the "repeated-word" variety or *kasane-kotoba*. In all of them, the first word is repeated, although sometimes with a phonetic change. (That is, *hōhō* becomes *hōbō*, *tokitoki* becomes *tokidoki,* and so on.)

Although there may be *kanji* for these adverbs (*hōbō* is 方々 and *tokidoki* is 時々), more often they are written in *kana*. Hundreds of these adverbs are in use, adding piquancy and color to everyday speech. Strangely, they are not given the attention they deserve in many textbooks.

Some of this class of adverbs are onomatopoetic in origin, as can be seen (or heard) in:

gorogoro   with a rumbling sound

gishigishi	with a creaking noise
hyūhyū	with a whistling sound
garagara	with a rattling sound (a *garagara-hebi* is a rattle-snake, *hebi* being the word for snake) *Garagara* also means empty, bare.
girigiri	the sound of teeth gnashing

To decide just how much these adverbs may sound like the actions they purport to describe may be difficult for Westerners, since certain universal phenomena apparently are heard differently by the Japanese. (To them, a dog barks *wan-wan;* to us it sounds more like bow-wow.) In any case, here are several more of these adverbs that may or may not be onomatopoetic.

zunzun	swiftly	*hōbō*	in all directions
tabitabi	often	*nikoniko*	smilingly
gungun	steadily	*hirahira*	in a fluttering
surasura	fluently		manner
nokonoko	unconcernedly	*suyasuya*	calmly (of sleep)
bikubiku	with trembling	*guruguru*	round and round
shimijimi	earnestly	*magomago*	in confusion
dondon	in rapid	*sorosoro*	slowly
	succession	*zorozoro*	in large groups

These *kasane-kotoba* will be taken up in more detail later in this course.

Tsumori (Intent)

When you wish to impart "I intend to—" or "I plan to—," say *tsumori desu* after the dictionary form of any verb.

Omae no sōshiki ni itte odoru tsumori da.
   I plan to go to your funeral and dance.
*Sakuban Mishima ni tatsu tsumori deshita ga...*I
   intended to leave for Mishima last night (but)...
Sono kirai na bōzu ni nido to au tsumori wa arimasen.
   I have no intention of meeting that hateful priest again.
Tsumori may also reflect a belief of the speaker:

Nyōbō wa go-jissai de ari-nagara mada wakai tsumori desu.
(Although my wife is fifty, she still thinks of herself as being young.)
Hachiuma ni mō kozukai wo yatta tsumori desu.
I believe I already gave Hachiuma his allowance. (*Kozukai* means both spending money and a servant. *Yaru* can mean to give—to an inferior—as well as To do. In the latter sense it is a synonym for *suru*.)
Yōchien teido no Eigo wa wakaru tsumori desu.
I believe I can understand kindergarten English. (*Teido* means 'level.')

-*nagara* (while, although)

-*nagara* is added to the basic stem of any verb to express the sense of 'while' or 'although.'

Terebi wo mi-nagara sembei wo tabemashita.
(I ate rice-crackers while watching television.)

Occasionally -*nagara* may be attached to adjectives as well as verbs.

Toboshii-nagara kawaisō na ko-neko ni esa wo yarimasu.
(Poor though I am, I will feed the pitiful kitten.)

-*nagara* is also used to mean 'while' in the sense of 'although,' just as we use it (mistakenly) in English. (See above sentence under *tsumori* re my aging wife.)

Kara (after, because)

Following verb forms, *kara* means 'because.'

Benkyō shite iru kara jama wo suru na.
(Because I am studying, don't bother me.)
Kinō wa atsukatta kara ichinichi pūru ni imashita.

(Because it was hot yesterday, I was in the pool all day.)

Nihongo wa muzukashii kara yonaka ni yoku nakimasu.

(Because Japanese is hard, I cry a lot at night.)

Shigoto ga nai kara jidōsha wo urimasu.

(Because I am out of work, I will sell my car.)

Sensei ga kibishii kara kanojo ni ringo wo ikko agemashō.

(Because the teacher is strict, let's give her an apple.)

But when *kara* is used after a gerund, the meaning becomes 'since' or 'after:'

Shigoto wo shite kara onna-asari ni dekakeyō.

(After work, let's go look for girls.) *Asaru* means to hunt for.

Nihongo no shiken ni rakudai shite kara, minna wa boku no kao wo mite warau. Since I failed the Japanese test, everyone looks at my face and laughs.

node (because, since)

Node is similar to the *kara* above, with one difference (see below). It can be used after verbs, nouns, or adjectives.

Kanojo-tachi wa sawagashii node minna ni mizu wo kakemashita.

(Because the women were noisy, I threw water on them.) Re this example sentence: although we might expect that the adjective for noisy would be in the past tense *(sawagashikatta)* rather than the present *(sawagashii),* in Japanese the tense of the final or principal predicate *(kakemashita)* does the job of telling the time of the action for both.

Eigo wa heta na node kōchō-san wa yoku domoru kuse ga arimasu. (Because his English is poor, the school principal has the habit of often stammering.) *Heta* is a B adjective that takes *na,* as shown in Lesson Four. Na is always used between such adjectives and *node. Domoru* is to mumble or stammer; *kuse* is a habit.

Asu wa saijitsu na node komban ōi ni asobimashō.

(Since tomorrow is a holiday, let's have a great time tonight.)

Yuki ga futta node zembu masshiroi desu.

(Everything is pure white, because snow has fallen.)

Okane ga nai kara ashita byōin ni itte ketsueki wo urimashō.

(Since I have no money, I will probably go to the hospital tomorrow and sell some blood.) In this sentence *kara* is used instead of *node* to emphasize the speaker's shortage of funds. Thus, *kara* usually emphasizes the reason while *node* emphasizes the result.

Kōhī wo nomanakatta node mada nemutai desu.

(I am still sleepy because I didn't drink my coffee.) *Node* is used in this sentence instead of *kara* to place emphasis on the result, e.g. the speaker's sleepiness.)

Naze ka to iu to (Because)

Naze ka to iu to is used at the beginning of a sentence and means 'because,' as in the second example below.

Naze kōhī ga hoshii to iwanakatta no desu ka.

(Why didn't you say you wanted some coffee?)

Naze ka to iu to o-isogashi-sō datta node....

(Because you seemed to be busy...) Note that the honorific *o* before the adjective *isogashii* (busy) shows that the speaker is talking about his listener instead of himself.

Cultural sidelights:

***While learning to acclimatize themselves in Japan's culture, foreigners must face the question of whether to bow and, if they bow, how deeply and how long. This is not a frivolous consideration, for it can result in embarrassment. One should bow when being introduced, when thanking another for a recent courtesy, and when apologizing. Women generally bow more deeply and more often than men, although age is a factor. It is appropriate to voice the amenities while bowing. *(Hajimete o-me ni kakarimasu, Senjitsu wa gochisō-sama deshita,* et al.) In fact, the last few words of these ritualistic phrases often trail off in the depth of the bow. Exactly how deeply to bow depends on age, position, and the circumstances, but a 90 degree bow may be excessive while a nod of the head may be too little. You should take care to watch your vis-a-vis out of the corner of an eye, so that your bow is of about the same duration as his. Since you are trying to adopt his custom while he may be trying to adopt yours, you may find yourself starting to bow just as the Japanese tries to shake your hand. There is no easy solution to this contretemps, but whatever you do, don't shake hands while bowing. That would be ludicrous. If the Japanese seems determined to shake hands, I suggest you follow suit, then bow to him on parting. To even the score.

Study recommendations: Stick to the regimen already laid out.

a. Keep pronunciation high among your priorities. Use whatever facilities are available to you to frequently monitor and improve your *hatsuon.* It will take much toil to master Japanese. Don't nullify your efforts with poor pronunciation.

b. Memorize the *bunkei!*

c. Make vocabulary cards for all the new words (and, soon, for the *kanji*) and review them often.

d. If you live in a Japanese community, watch Japanese television, listen to the Japanese radio, see Japanese movies, associate mostly with Japanese, shun the islands of foreign culture, and *ask* when you don't understand.

e. Speak Japanese clearly and with confidence (even when you may quail inwardly). Damn the mistakes. Full steam ahead!

f. Be serious about your studies. If your intent is just to learn enough Japanese to amuse your friends, I advise you to change your major to Spanish. Learning Japanese will be hard work, but it will have its rewards. (At least, that's what I have been telling myself for the past forty-nine years.)

Lesson Ten

A.) *Noni, tame ni*—In order to
B.) *Noni*—Even though
C.) *Tokoro*—Place, time, et al
D.) *Dokoro ka*—Quite the contrary...
E.) *-tari (-dari) suru*—to do this and that
F.) *Hō ga ii...* It is better to...
G.) Numerators
H.) Passive Voice
I.) The Causative and the Passive Causative

Useful Everyday Expressions

Dōzo go-enryo naku...   Please don't stand on ceremony. Lit., Please ...honorable reserve...without...

Jā, izure mata...   Well, so long...Lit., Well, anyway again...Men only should use this with male friends who are approximate equals.

Kokoro bakari desu ga.... It's merely a token, but (please accept it). Lit., Heart...only...is but...Said when handing someone a present.

Kekkō na shina wo itadaite...
    (Thanks) for this fine present. Lit., Fine merchandise receiving...

O-tanoshimi desu, ne.   You must be looking forward to it. Or, you must be enjoying it.

Kochira koso.   No, I'm the one who should be saying that. Lit., This way, indeed...Often said in answer to words of thanks or apology by another.

Zannen desu, ne.   That's too bad. Said when both parties to a dialog are disappointed about some event.

Gomen nasai.   Pardon me. Excuse me. *Go* is honorific, *men* is face, and *nasai* is the imperative of the polite verb *nasaru,* to do. *Gomen nasai* sounds a little childish or feminine and is used mostly among family members or by women when speaking to other women or children.

124

Gomen kudasai.	Whereas *Gomen nasai* is an apology, *Gomen kudasai* is a greeting. When entering the *genkan* of a home, you should call out, *Gomen kudasai!* When someone appears and asks you to enter, you should then say *Shitsurei shimasu.* When leaving, however, you may say either of the two—with a bow, of course.
	Gomen kudasai is also said when you are about to end a telephone conversation.
Ē, chotto...	Yes, just a little...This may be said when you wish to admit to some discomfort or inconvenience. "Are you too hot?" *"Ē, chotto..."*
Chotto!	Come here just a moment! Used when calling a waiter to your table or when you want your wife to fetch something for you.
O-ki ni irimashita ka.	Do (did) you like it? Lit., Did it enter your honorable spirit?

Vocabulary

saifu	purse, wallet	*okoru*	to occur, as an earthquake or event
tame	in order to		
no tame ni	for the sake of		
yubi	finger	*keru*	to kick
yubiwa	ring	*undōka*	athlete
hōchō	kitchen knife	*shinshi*	gentleman
Seisho	Bible (Christian)	*suku*	to become empty (v.i.)
jitensha	bicycle		
kasu	to lend	*zama*	predicament
kariru	to borrow	*ayamaru*	to apologize
kokoro	heart	*ginkō*	bank
Hora!	Look!	*o-mawari-san*	policeman
yoru	night	*happa*	leaf
yoru	to stop by (v.i.)	*ireba*	false teeth (tooth)
yakunin	official	*kimba*	gold teeth (tooth)
rakudai suru	to fail	*tamaranai*	to be unbearable
utsu	to hit, to shoot	*nusumu*	to steal
jishin	earthquake	*izure*	anyhow

ōmu	parrot	*shitsugyō*	
mei	niece	*suru*	to be out of work
oi	nephew	*rippa (na)*	fine, splendid
hitoban-jū	all night long	*enzetsu*	speech
zeimusho	tax office	*sōri-daijin*	prime minister
teppō	rifle	*keshikaran*	inexcusable, damnable
kasegu	to earn	*nara*	if (after the present
zannen	regrettable		and past tenses of
tanoshimi	pleasure		verbs)
shina (or	merchandise,	*tamago*	egg
shinamono)	goods	*yaru*	
keshiki	scenery	*kureru*	
suru to	in that case	*ageru*	to give (see
gyaku ni	in contrast with	*sashiageru*	Cultural
	this	*ataeru*	Sidelights)
		kamu	to bite

Pattern Sentences

(Bunkei)

1. *Ki ni shinaide kudasai.* — Never mind. Don't let it bother you. (Note difference between this and *ki ga suru,* to have the feeling that...)

2. *Ayamaru dokoro ka.* — Me, apologize? (I should think not!)

3. *Ii zama da.* — Serves (him) right. Lit., Good...predicament—is. Rough and spiteful in tone.

4. *Zama miro!* — Serves (him) right! Lit., Look at what a mess (he) is in. Because *miro* is the rough imperative of the verb *miru,* to see, this is even harsher than *Bunkei* No. 3 above.

5. *Eki ni itte kudasai.* — Please go to the station. (What you might tell a cab driver.)

6. *Dorobō wo ginkō no naka ni hairasenai hō ga ii desu.* — It would be better not to let the robber go inside the bank.

7. *Ame ni furaremashita.* — I got rained on.

8. *Sono chiisai kodomo ni mo* Are you going to let even that little
    o-sake wo nomasemasu ka. child drink rice-wine?
9. *Sono ato tonari no inu wa* After that, the neighbor's dog was bitten
    kodomo ni kamaremashita. by the child.
10. *Naze kamimashita ka.* Why did (he) bite (the dog)?
11. *O-naka ga suite tamara-* Because (he) was so hungry, (he) could
    nakatta kara desu. not stand it.
12. *Naze obāsama no ireba wo* Why are you going to sell grandmother's
    uru ndesu ka. Kimba to false teeth? They're not gold. (Note the
    chigaimasu yo. *n* prefixed to *desu,* a contraction of *no*
    that does not change the meaning.)
13. *Otaku no mina-san wa* All the people in your house are good
    bakuchi ga o-jōzu desu ne. gamblers, aren't they. *Otaku* is honor-
    able house or your house. It may also
    be used to refer to the company employ-
    ing the other person. Sometimes it can
    mean 'you' if you don't know the other
    person's name or title. In this sense, it is
    impersonal. And although not rude, it
    doesn't impart a feeling of warm respect.
14. *Sore, kudasai.* Let me have that. (See Cultural Side-
    lights.)

How to Use
Noni, tame ni—In order to

'In order to' can be expressed by adding *noni* or *tame ni* to the
dictionary form of a verb.

O-kane wo kasegu noni, ningen wa hatarakimasu. In order to
earn money, people work.
Raishū Fuji-san ni noboru tame ni kyō kara jūbun ni yasumi-
mashō. In order to climb Mt. Fuji next week, let's get enough
rest from today on.

Tame or *tame ni* basically means 'for the sake of.' *Kanojo no tame*
ni nan de mo shimasu. I will do anything for her sake.

Nan no tame ni konna tokoro ni kimashita ka. Why (for the sake of what) did (you) come to this kind of place?

On occasion, *tame* or *tame ni* can be used to mean 'because.'

Yūbe biiru ya o-sake wo issho ni nonda tame, kesa atama ga itai ndesu. Because I drank beer and sake together last night, this morning my head hurts.

Noni— Even though

After present tense and past tense verbs and adjectives, *noni* can also carry the meaning of 'even though' or 'in spite of the fact that.'

Atsui noni sono Indo-jin wa ōbā wo kite imasu.
Even though it is hot, that Indian is wearing an overcoat.

Hontō no koto wo itta noni donata mo shinjimasen deshita.
Although I spoke the truth (said true things), no one believed me.

Sensei wa rippa na shinshi da to hometa noni watakushi wa rakudai shimashita. Despite the fact that I praised the teacher as a fine gentleman, I failed (the course).

Noni also expresses—usually about the second or third person—a lack of expectation. For instance,

Hontō ni gonen-kan shitsugyō shite imasu ka. Have you really been unemployed for five years? *Shigoto wo sagaseba ii noni...* You should look for a job (but)... Lit., Job (or work)...if search for...would be good (but)...Implicit is the resignation that the unemployed lay-about won't get off his duff.

Tokoro

Tokoro (所) can mean point, part, time, home, or occasion, but its fundamental meaning is 'place.' Quite often the Japanese use it to mean house or home or place of business.

> *Ano kata no tokoro ni yotte kara hikōjō ni mairimasu.*
> I will go to the airport after dropping by that person's home.

In fact, a word for address is *tokoro-banchi* or place-number.

Just as often, *tokoro* can mean a specific time or occasion:

Neru tokoro desu.	I am just on the point of going to bed (sleeping).
Ofuro ni haitta tokoro jishin ga okorimashita.	Just when I had entered the bath, the earthquake struck.
Anata no shiru tokoro de wa arimasen.	That is none of your business. (Here *tokoro* is more like a 'matter.')
Sensei no kaita hon wo yonde ita tokoro desu.	I was just reading the book the teacher wrote.
Kuruma ni notta tokoro nyōbō ga watakushi wo tomemashita.	My wife stopped me just as I got into the car.

There is a chance for confusion here, so take care. This sentence can have two meanings:

Fune ga nyūkō suru to-koro wo mimashita.	This can mean either "I saw the ship (in the act of) coming in," or "I saw where the ship comes in to port."

Dokoro ka

By saying *dokoro ka* after the present or past tense of a verb, you contradict the meaning of the verb.

Hanasu dokoro ka. Kusuri mo nomenai hodo nodo ga itai desu.
Speak? Why, my throat is so sore I can't even swallow medicine.
O-kane wo kasu dokoro ka. Anata kara karitai desu.
Far from lending you money, I'd like to borrow (some) from you.

—*tari (-dari) suru*—To do this and that

Add *-ri* to the plain past tense of a verb, do the same to another verb, and follow them with a form of the verb *suru* (to do):

Otōto wo kettari uttari shite imasu.
(He) is kicking and hitting (his) younger brother.
Kisha no naka de keshiki wo mitari zasshi wo yondari shima-shita. Aboard the train I looked at the scenery and read magazines.

Sometimes only one *-tari (-dari)* is used.

As, *Konya sampo shitari shite jikan wo sugoshimasu.* Tonight I will go for a walk (and do other things) to pass the time.

-tari (-dari) can mean doing two things at once (eating and reading), doing things in alternation, or doing this and that and perhaps something else later.

Hō ga ii—It is better to—

Hō is a noun that means either direction or choice of, but it is often used in a way that may seem superfluous to newcomers. For instance, *Ane no hō ga sei ga takai desu.* Elder sister's 'direction'... as for...stature...high...is. Or, My older sister is taller. However, if we omitted *hō,* then the meaning would become simply, My older sister is tall. By introducing *hō,* we put across the idea that there is a comparison.

By adding *hō ga ii* to the dictionary form of a verb or the plain past tense, we are enabled to say, It is better to (do this) or (say that). Or, with the negative present tense, It is better not to (do this) or (say that).

> *Gakkō ni hashitte itta hō ga ii desu.*
> You should (It is better to) run to school.
> *Doa wo shimeru hō ga ii deshō.*
> It is probably better to close the door.
> *Ano o-mawari-san wo ijimenai hō ga ii desu.*
> It is better not to torment that policeman.

Occasionally you will hear the *hō* omitted in such expressions. Instead of:

> *Hayaku ojisan ni ayamatta hō ga ii desu.*
> You should apologize to your uncle quickly.

You will hear the *hō* omitted:

> *Hayaku ojisan ni ayamaru ga ii desu.*
> You should apologize to your uncle quickly.

When expressing a choice, *hō* may also be preceded by an adjective. "Do you like it hot or cold?"

> *Atsui hō ga ii desu.*
> I like it hot. Lit., Hot direction, as for...good...is.

Bear in mind that verbs followed by *hō ga ii* should usually refer to others, not to yourself. Suppose you are seated in a conference and decide you would like to stand up. If you say, *Sā, tatta hō ga ii* (Well, it's better to stand up), the other attendees are liable to come to their feet, too. Instead, you should have said, *Sā, tachimashō* (Well, I'm going to stand up), then go on with whatever it was you had in mind.

Numerators

It is with a heavy heart that I come to the subject of numerators (or numeratives or counters). The numbers were bad enough; the numerators are worse. There is, however, no help for it, so let us press ahead with steely determination.

Until now, you may have been using the 'native' numbers to count objects: *nanatsu no Seisho* (seven Bibles), *yottsu no teppō* (four rifles), and *futatsu no jitensha* (two bicycles). If so, it is now time to progress to adult mathematics and learn the numbing numerators.

What you will meet here is a reasonably complete list of those numerators in common use today. There are more, but most are archaic or obsolescent and can be ignored.

Numerator	Objects counted
chaku	suits, dresses
chō	scissors, knives, pistols, saws, and bladed objects with handles
dai	typewriters, pianos, beds, vehicles (except aircraft, which are counted *ikki, niki, sanki,* etc., and ships, which are noted below). *Dai,* in addition to *sei* (as in *nisei* and *sansei*), is also used to count generations, although the *kanji* is different.
fuku	doses of medicine, puffs of tobacco smoke
hai	cups, glasses, bucketfuls, etc. of liquid
hiki	quadrupeds, insects, fish (*bi* is an older numerator for fish)
hon	things somewhat rounded and long in proportion to their thickness, such as trees, cigarettes, ropes, teeth, fans, legs, needles, pencils, cigars, bottles, fingers, poles
jō	*tatami* mats, batches of twenty sheets of dried, edible seaweed (written with a different *kanji*), quires of paper
kan	reels or a movie, individual volumes in a set of books
ken	houses, shops, buildings
ko	various objects for which there are no numerators

mai	flat things, e.g., boards, paper, dishes, kimono, blankets
maki	rolls of silk and other cloth, scrolls
mei	persons. A more formal or literary way of counting persons than *nin* (see below).
mon	cannons
nin	persons
satsu	books, magazines
seki	large ships
sho	places
shu	poems
sō	small ships (although this may be used for ships as large as submarines)
soku	footwear: pairs of shoes, *geta,* socks, *tabi, zōri*
tō	large quadrupeds, whales
tsū	letters and documents
wa	birds
zen	rice bowls, pairs of chopsticks

The Chinese numbers (*ichi, ni, san, shi* or *yon, go,* and so forth) are those used in most cases with the numerators. When the number and the numerator are combined, phonetic changes often take place. For instance, *ichi* (one) and *-chaku* (for dresses and suits) are not spoken as *ichi-chaku* but as *itchaku.* There are many such changes and the rules that govern them, but I believe it is easier to memorize the following table. This will save you the trouble of dredging up the rule from your memory bank each time you have to count something.

To be sure, memorizing this table won't be an *asa-meshi mae no shigoto* (a before-breakfast chore—or something easy to do), but maybe if you take it a little at a time and make some vocabulary cards...

Number-Numerator Combinations

Numer-ator	Combined with Numbers											How Many?
	1	2	3	4	5	6	7	8	9	10	100	
chaku	itchaku	nichaku	sanchaku	yonchaku	gochaku	rokuchaku	nanachaku	hatchaku	kyūchaku	jitchaku	hyakuchaku	nanchaku
chō	itchō	nichō	sanchō	yonchō	gochō	rokuchō	shichichō nanchō	hatchō	kyūchō	jitchō	hyakuchō	nanchō
dai	ichidai	nidai	sandai	yodai yondai	godai	rokudai	shichidai nanadai	hachidai	kudai kyūdai	jūdai	hyakudai	nandai
fuku	ippuku	nifuku	sampuku sambuku	yompuku shifuku	gofuku	roppuku	shichifuku nanafuku	happuku	kyūfuku	jippuku	hyappuku	nampuku nambuku
hai	ippai	nihai	sambai	yonhai shihai	gohai	roppai	shichihai	hachihai happai	kuhai kyūhai	jippai	hyappai	nambai
hiki	ippiki	nihiki	sambiki	yonhiki shihiki	gohiki	roppiki	shichihiki nanahiki	hachihiki happiki	kuhiki kyūhiki	jippiki	hyappiki	nambiki
hon	ippon	nihon	sambon	yonhon shihon	gohon	roppon	shichihon nanahon	hachihon happon	kuhon kyūhon	jippon	hyappon	nambon
jō	ichijō	nijō	sanjō	yojō	gojō	rokujō	shichijō nanjō	hachijō	kujō kyūjō	jūjō	hyakujō	nanjō
kan	ikkan	nikan	sangan	yonkan	gokan	rokkan	shichikan nanakan	hachikan hakkan	kyūkan	jikkan	hyakkan	nangan
ken	ikken	niken	sangen	yonken shiken	goken	rokken	shichiken nanaken	hachiken hakken	kyūken	jikken	hyakken	nangen
ko	ikko	niko	sanko	yonko	goko	rokko	shichiko nanako	hakko	kyūko	jikko	hyakko	nanko
mai	ichimai	nimai	sammai	yomai yommai	gomai	rokumai	shichimai nanamai	hachimai	kumai kyūmai	jūmai	hyakumai	nammai

maki	hitomaki	futamaki	mimaki	yomaki	itsumaki	mumaki	nanamaki	yamaki	kyūmaki	tomaki	hyakumaki	nammaki
mei	ichimei	nimei	sammei	yomei yommei shimei	gomei	rokumei	shichimei nanamei	hachimei	kumei kyūmei	jūmei	hyakumei	nammei
mon	ichimon	nimon	sammon	yommon	gomon	rokumon	shichimon nanamon	hachimon	kumon kyūmon	jūmon	hyakumon	nammon
nin	hitori	futari	sannin	yonin yottari	gonin	rokunin	shichinin	hachinin	kunin kyūnin	jūnin	hyakunin	nannin
satsu	issatsu	nisatsu	sansatsu	yonsatsu shisatsu	gosatsu	rokusatsu	shichisatsu nanasatsu	hassatsu	kyūsatsu	jissatsu	hyakusatsu	nansatsu
seki	isseki	niseki	sanseki	yonseki	goseki	rokuseki	shichiseki nanaseki	hasseki	kyūseki	jisseki	hyakuseki	nanseki
sho	ikkasho	nikasho	sankasho	yonkasho	gokasho	rokkasho	nanakasho	hachikasho	kyūkasho	jikkasho	hyakkasho	nankasho
shu	isshu	nishu	sanshu	yonshu	goshu	rokushu	shichishu	hachishu hasshu	kyūshu	jisshu	hyakushu	nanshu
sō	issō	nisō	sansō sanzō	yonsō shisō	gosō	rokusō	shichisō nanasō	hassō	kyūsō	jissō	hyakusō	nansō nanzō
soku	issoku	nisoku	sanzoku	yonsoku shisoku	gosoku	rokusoku	shichisoku nanasoku	hassoku	kyūsoku	jissoku	hyakusoku	nanzoku
tō	ittō	nitō	santō	yontō	gotō	rokutō	shichitō nanatō	hachitō hattō	kyūtō	jittō	hyakutō	nantō
tsū	ittsū	nitsū	santsū	yontsū shitsū	gotsū	rokutsū	shichitsū nanatsū	hachitsū hattsū	kyūtsū	jittsū	hyakutsū	nantsū
wa	ichiwa	niwa	samba	yonwa yomba shiwa	gowa	roppa rokuwa	shichiwa	hachiwa	kuwa kyūwa	jippa	hyappa	namba
zen	ichizen	nizen	sanzen	yonzen shizen	gozen	rokuzen	shichizen nanazen	hachizen	kyūzen	jūzen	hyakuzen	nanzen

The Passive Voice

The passive voice is not used as much in Japanese as in English. Usually, where in English we would use the passive voice in a relative clause...

The purse that was stolen by the thief

...the Japanese will change the verb to the active voice:

> *Dorobō ga nusunda saifu*
> (Lit., Thief—as for—stole—purse.)

In English, we have a regrettable tendency to use the passive voice in order to sound scholarly. Such pretentious speakers will often say something like, "Progress has been made," when "We have made progress" would be more effective. This usage, however, is not at all common in Japanese.

In Japanese, the passive voice is most often used about people, especially the speakers, and indicates the speaker's feelings, often negative, about what was done to him, as we shall see.

With Conjugation A verbs (see Lesson Six), the passive voice is formed by adding *-reru* to the negative stem.

Dictionary form	Negative stem	Passive voice
kau (to buy)	*kawa-*	*kawareru* (to be bought)
motsu (to hold, have)	*mota-*	*motareru* (to be held)
dasu (to put out)	*dasa-*	*dasareru* (to be put out)

With Conjugation B verbs (see Lesson Seven), the passive voice is formed by adding *-rareru* to the negative stem.

Dictionary form	Negative stem	Passive voice
wasureru (to forget)	*wasure-*	*wasurerareru* (to be forgotten)
okiru (to arise)	*oki-*	*okirareru* (to be arisen —see below)

Oddly—to us, at least—many intransitive as well as transitive verbs have passive forms in Japanese.

Intransitive verb	Passive voice	Usage
furu (to fall)	*furareru*	*yuki ni furareru* (to be fallen on by snow)
shinu (to die)	*shinareru*	*Uchi no ōmu ni shinareta.* (Our parrot died on us.)

Often, as in the usage immediately above, the sense is one of something having happened that one wishes had not happened.

The passive forms of irregular verbs are:

kuru (to come)	*korareru*
iru (to be)	*irareru*
suru (to do)	*sareru*

The standard form for the passive voice with the various applicable particles is shown in this sentence:

Watakushi wa mei ni te wo hōchō de kirareta (kiraremashita).
I had my hand cut by my niece with a butcher knife.

In English, we would have said, My hand was cut by my niece with a butcher knife, which would be directly translated into Japanese as, *Watakushi no te ga mei ni hōchō de kiraremashita.* Although this is grammatically correct, the Japanese would usually say (in addition to dropping *watakushi no*), *Mei ni te wo hōchō de kiraremashita.* Whereas in English the word hand *(te)* becomes the subject of the passive verb 'to be cut', in Japanese it often remains the direct object of the verb even in the passive voice.

Both are correct, but *te wo* is more common than *te ga*.

The person doing the action is indicated by the postpositional particle *ni* (equivalent to the English 'by'), although at times *kara* may be used instead.

> *Chichi kara* (instead of *ni*) *shikararemashita.*
> I was scolded by my father.
> *Zeimusho no keshikaran yakunin ni zeikin wo hyakuman-en toraremashita. Tonde mo nai hanashi desu.* The insolent officials at the tax office have taken one million yen in taxes (from me). What a ridiculous story! (Here again we see the use of *wo* after *zeikin* instead of *ga*.)

The passive voice in Japanese can be used as a polite manner of speech.

> *Nihon no sōri-daijin ga konya no hachiji ni enzetsu wo saremasu.*
> Japan's prime minister will make a speech tonight at eight o'clock.

This usage is generally restricted to official announcements and public speeches and is used more often by men than by women.

An equivalent form in ordinary speech is to prefix the basic stem of the verb with the honorific *o* and to follow it with *ni naru (ni narimasu)*.

> *o-suwari ni naru (narimasu)*   to sit
> *o-hanashi ni naru (narimasu)*   to speak
> *o-odori ni naru (narimasu)*   to dance

The Causative and the Passive Causative

The causative form of the verb is that in which a person causes another to take an action. In the case of Conjugation A verbs, it is constructed by attaching *-seru* to the negative stem.

au (to meet)	*awaseru* (to cause to meet)
naku (to cry)	*nakaseru* (to cause to cry)
motsu (to hold)	*motaseru* (to cause to hold)

With the Conjugation B verbs, the causative is formed by suffixing *-saseru* to the negative stem.

| *miseru* (to show) | *misesaseru* (to cause to show) |
| *yameru* (to stop) | *yamesaseru* (to cause to stop) |

Sometimes, with verbs like *okiru* (to get up), there is already a verb *(okosu —to* arouse, to cause to get up) that is used in place of the causative form *(okisaseru).* The *kanji* are the same, so both verbs have the same root.

The person who is caused to take some action can be indicated by the postpositional *ni,* as in:

> *Haha wa tomodachi ni uta wo utawasemashita.*
> My mother had her friend sing a song.

This causative form of a verb is, by and large, used when someone can order or permit an act by another. If, however, an action is performed out of kindness, such forms as *itte itadaku* (to have someone go—as a favor) or, less politely, *itte morau* (to have someone go—again, as a favor) are used. Example:

> *Kinjo no o-toshiyori ni itte itadakimashita.*
> I had an older person in the neighborhood go for me.

Perhaps this chart will help fix these constructions in your mind:

Conjugation A Verb	Negative Stem	Causative	Passive	Causative Passive
ugokasu	*ugokasa-*	*ugokasaseru*	*ugokasa-reru*	*ugokasaserareru*

Conjugation B Verb	Negative Stem	Causative	Passive	Causative Passive
hajimeru	*hajime-*	*hajimesa-seru*	*hajime-rareru*	*hajimesasera-reru*

The inflections of the two irregular verbs *kuru* (to come) and *suru* (to do) follow:

kuru	to come
kosaseru	to cause to come
kosaseyō	will probably cause to come
kosasereba or kosasetara	if (or when) (you) cause to come
kosasetari	causing to come (and do other things).
suru	to do
saseru	to cause to do
saserareyō	will probably be caused to do
saseraretara or saserarereba	if (or when) caused to do
saseraretari	being caused to do this and that

Cultural sidelights:

*** In American English these troubled days, we often hear the phrase "No problem" used to mean "Don't mention it." The unwary may be tempted to learn the Japanese word for problem—*mondai*—and use it in a somewhat similar fashion. (Don't do it.) Or to say, *Mondai ga arimasu* to mean 'I have a problem.' If the problem really is one of significant dimensions, that is all right. But the Japanese avoid that usage unless such is the case.

Not only that but *mondai* may suggest adverse criticism, whereas Americans may use the word 'problem' no matter who is at fault or even when no one is at fault or even if our right knee itches.

Mondai is often used to mean a "Question" on school examination papers.

*** In the Vocabulary, five verbs are listed with the meaning of "to give." There are, needless to say, others. For the present, just remember *ageru* (to give, to lift up to) as the polite word you should usually use. *Sashiageru* is a degree politer. *Yaru* may be used with an intimate friend or someone below you. *Kureru* is used when someone else gives you or someone in your family something. (*Ano shinsetsu na Kankoku-jin ga imōto ni kawaii ko-neko wo kuremashita.* That kind Korean gave my younger sister a cute kitten.) *Ataeru* is more formal and less conscious of social rankings.

*** The last of the *bunkei* above is what you might say when you see something in a store you want. In English, in buying situations, we—reasonably—use the verb 'to buy.' ("I'll buy that," "Let me buy that," and so forth.) The Japanese, however, tend to avoid saying *kau* (to buy), probably because monetary transactions are played down in Japan. Like belching, purchases are necessary parts of life, but the Japanese feel that we don't have to be so blatant about it.

In the same way, "give" should be avoided, where possible, in direct situations. Instead of saying, "I give you this watch," try to express the meaning in other ways. ("Please accept this Rolex." "This is a mere token (but)..." "I hope it keeps time.")

For years I chided my Japanese wife because when she gave a gift to someone, she often prefixed the words, "This is something we really don't need any more." She made it sound as if she were giving away junk. At length, she persuaded me, however, that this is proper in Japan because by giving something that is of no account, you are lessening the *on* (burden) on the recipient to respond with a gift of value.

Study recommendations:

It has been my experience that the Japanese (except your teachers in the classroom) will never correct your mistakes. Nor can you immediately ask everyone you meet to do that chore for you. Therefore, I suggest that you select two or three (or more) close friends and explain to them—earnestly and in detail—that you are in urgent need of someone to point out your mistakes in pronunciation, grammar, and word meanings; that you will not only forgive them this discourtesy but that you will forever be in their debt. Even so, it will probably be hard for them to do something that is so contrary to their nature, so for a while thereafter, you should remind them several times during each dialog: "Did I say that right?" "How was my pronunciation?" and so forth.

Lesson Eleven

Kanji (the written characters)

Japanese is usually written from top to bottom and from right to left.

日本語
と英語

Occasionally, however, Japanese may be written horizontally and from left to right, in the same way as English.

日本語と英語

The actual writing (with brush or pen, called the stroke order) combines the above, in that the strokes are written from top to bottom but from left to right.

In textbooks, this stroke order may be shown by adding one stroke at a time with arrows showing the correct stroke direction:

丨 冂 月 日

Or by numbering the strokes:

Stroke order is of supreme importance. Some students have learned to write *kanji* with their own self-designed stroke order, which is difficult to correct once it is implanted. The correct order is the most efficient and natural. To "impress it on your liver" *(kimo ni meijiru),* I recommend writing each new *kanji* 100 times. Only then will you begin to feel the natural flow of the strokes.

In Defense of *Kanji*

At first acquaintance, the *kanji* may seem like the disorderly tracks of a tipsy chicken, and no one will seriously challenge the notion that they are a formidable barrier in the student's path. Efforts have been made to abolish them, but without success—for the Japanese have used them for more than 1,500 years. With almost 100 percent literacy, they support their way of writing with reasons that deserve respect.

Westerners may make the mistake of thinking of the 1,945 *"Kanji for Daily Use" (Tōyō Kanji)* as a kind of alphabet and bemoan having to learn so many 'symbols,' whereas the English alphabet contains only twenty-six letters. Yet it is the *kana* syllabaries that are the Japanese alphabets while the *kanji* are words in themselves— or the building blocks of a great many compound words. In this sense, the *kanji* could be better compared to the Greek and Latin (and German and French) words—of which there are thousands— that are the foundations of English. When you have learned a *kanji* like 人 (person), you have learned a word, not a letter.

Some think that because of the apparent complexity of the *kanji,* it must take much longer to write a thought in these ideograms than in English. Not necessarily. A typical *kanji* may contain seven or eight strokes while the average number of "strokes" in a printed

English word may be about the same. The above *kanji* for *hito* or person has two strokes— 丿 and 乀 that result in 人, but if you print 'person', you will use twelve separate marks. (To be sure, there are many examples of multi-stroked *kanji* with short English equivalents.)

One cogent argument in favor of the "tersely-expressive" *kanji* involves the pictorial nature of their origins, and it has been demonstrated that between seven and eleven percent of American school children have significant difficulty in learning to read while the comparable figure for the Japanese is less than one percent. A reason for our poor showing is the abstract nature of our alphabet. American children have to learn that the letter 'a' stands for certain sounds, although they can see no apparent connection between these sounds and the letter. In Japanese, however, the *kanji* for fish *(sakana)* bears a certain resemblance to a fish, as we can see in the historical development of that *kanji:*

In English, we also have the problem of mirror-image letters such as b and d, q and g and words such as was and saw, on and no, and felt and left.

In Japanese, often the *kanji* are directly descended from pictures of the objects themselves. See how these pictograms evolved: 𪨊 to 𡸴 to 山, meaning mountain. From ⊙ to ⊖ to ⊖ to 日 meaning sun. From 朩 to 木, meaning tree. From 🔲 to 𠕎 to 雨, meaning rain.

Often, two of these primitive pictograms were combined to communicate an abstract thought. For instance, the *kanji* for sun (日) was combined with the *kanji* for moon (月) to form a character (明) for "bright." What could be brighter than the rays of both the sun and the moon?

To be sure, the etymology of the *kanji* is not always so apparent. Take, for example, a single *kanji* for marriage: 婚. The left part is the radical for woman (女) while the right portion is 昏 for night *(kon)*. Why does a "woman at night" mean marriage? Because at some time in China's distant, enlightened past, men used the cover of darkness to seize and make off with desired women. Such etymology, though valid, is not known to the average user of *kanji* today, so it does the student little good, but at least the presence of the woman 'radical' (女) in this *kanji* may offer a clue to the area of meaning.

Kanji are also useful as building blocks in the many compound words used by the Japanese. I have had the experience of seeing a rare scientific word in English by the side of its Japanese equivalent and comprehending the meaning from the Japanese *kanji*, whereas the English word was meaningless to me. The first of many illustrations that crowd to mind is 'pseudocyesis' and its Japanese translation, 想像妊娠 *(sōzō-ninshin)*. I had no idea what the former meant, but the meaning of the latter was immediately apparent: *Sōzō* is imagination and *ninshin* is pregnancy. Imagined pregnancy or, according to a medical lexicon, false pregnancy.

Then there was the English 'agoraphobia' next to the Japanese 広場恐怖症 *(hiroba-kyōfushō)*. A glance at the *kanji* told me that this meant a fear of open spaces, although I would have had to use a dictionary to acquaint myself with the meaning of agoraphobia. I could hunt up hundreds of such examples, I am sure.

These building blocks are far more familiar to the Japanese than most of the Greek and Latin words on which English is based are to us. So familiar, in fact, that the Japanese can even construct their own compounds. Only the other day, my Japanese wife and I were talking about our family dog, and I said, *Uchi no inu wa guken ka kenken ka shira?* Well, the only *guken* in my Kenkyusha dictionary is the one meaning 'my view,' and there is no *kenken,* but my stalwart frau knew immediately that by *guken ka kenken,* I meant 'dumb dog or smart dog,' because of her visual *and* aural familiarity with the 'building blocks' in each word:　愚犬か賢犬.

Kanji Structure

Kanji are written with the 214 historic 'radicals' or parts. These are to be found on the left, the right, the top, and the bottom. If on the left, they are called *hen,* as in *onna-hen* (扌) or the woman radical. If on the right, they are called *tsukuri,* as in *ōzato-zukuri* (阝) or the large village radical. If on top, they are called *kammuri,* as in *u-kammuri* (宀) or the *u* radical from its resemblance to the *katakana* symbol *u* (ウ).

Although radicals may constitute the bottom portion of a *kanji,* none are used there exclusively, so no particular name is given to those in that position.

All the radicals have designations in Japanese, as shown above. If you would find it easier to work with English descriptions, the earlier-mentioned Nelson's dictionary gives English "nicknames" for them.

In most *kanji* dictionaries, the characters are arranged by radical and number of strokes. Suppose you want to know the meaning of the *kanji* 軒. The left-hand side of this character (車) is *kuruma-hen* or the vehicle radical. Turning to the radical chart at the front of Nelson's dictionary, you will find that this radical is number 159, which enables you to look it up. (The radicals are numbered 1 through 214.)

Now you will see there are six pages of *kanji* with this vehicle radical, including their compounds. Next, you would count the number of strokes in the rest of the *kanji* (in this case three), and you will find what you are looking for on the first page. In short, it is a vehicle-radical *kanji* with three additional strokes.

Many radicals can be used alone as complete *kanji;* some cannot. But such *kanji* may change form somewhat when they join with another radical to form a different *kanji.* A handy example is the character for water. Standing alone, it is 水. As a radical, however, it becomes 氵.

Because they have meanings themselves, the radicals may give a hint as to the meaning of the *kanji* in question. Whenever you come across a *kanji* with the tree radical (木), you can start your search for the meaning from the hope that it may be something made of wood or perhaps a kind of wood or tree. To be sure, this does not necessarily always hold true, for you will come up against a tree-radical *kanji* like 検 *(ken),* meaning investigation. Perhaps in the distant past the village magistrate responsible for criminal investigations may have employed a wooden staff as his symbol of authority or he might have held court under a certain tree. Whatever the etymology, it is of little use to the student today.

When I look over the several *kanji* with the above vehicle-radical (車), I find a variety of meanings that have little or no apparent connection with vehicles: beheading, soft, sadness, trifling, comparison, helping, collection, wedge, and misfortune.

In summary, the meaning of the radical may sometimes help—but certainly not always.

The Mix of *Kanji* and *Kana*

When you study the make-up of a Japanese sentence, you will see that the nouns, verb stems, and adjective bases are given in *kanji,* while the particles, connectives, suffixes, prefixes, copulas, and verb and adjective endings are written in *kana.* Adverbs and pronouns seem to be written in either these days.

In a specific example, take the sentence, *Watakushi wa yoku Tōkyō ni ikimasu* or 私は良く東京に行きます. (I go to Tokyo often.) The *kanji* in this sentence are the pronoun *watakushi* (私), the adverb base *yo-* (良), the place name *Tōkyō* (東京), and the verb stem *iki-* (行). The *kana* are the post-positional particle *wa* (は) that indicates the subject, the suffix of the adverb *-ku* (く), the particle *ni* (に) meaning 'to,' and the polite verb ending *-masu* (-ます). The pronoun subject could have been represented in *kana,* although it would usually be *watashi* (わたし) instead of *watakushi* (わたくし), which is older and somewhat stiffer in tone. The adverb *yoku* is more often written in *kana* (よく).

An analogy might be found in the structure of a house, with the foundation, roof, and frame being the *kanji,* and the fixtures, flooring, siding, windows, and paint being the *kana.*

According to the National Language Research Institute, *kanji* make up 41.3 percent of all the written symbols in Japanese, with the *kana* accounting for the rest.

The same Institute also has found that words of Chinese origin make up about 48 percent of the Japanese language (that is, dictionary entries) while words of Japanese origin account for about 37 percent. (The remainder are *gairaigo* or imported words.) Even so, in everyday speech words of Japanese origin are used more frequently. This is understandable since the words from China tend to be more scholarly.

Kinds of *Kanji*

There are several different kinds of *kanji.* Some are close to the original pictograms; others are used for their sound only with no relation to their original meaning. A few were concocted in Japan and so have only Japanese *(kun)* readings and no Chinese *(on)* readings. But about 90% percent of the *kanji* are combinations of a part that was originally chosen for its meaning and a part that was chosen for its pronuciation.

Kanji Readings

How a *kanji* is pronounced or 'read' is most important. A character may have only one reading or it may have a dozen or more. The average has two: the *on* (or Chinese) and the *kun* (or Japanese) reading.

When the Japanese began adopting Chinese writing, their scholars would take a particular *kanji,* whose Chinese reading and meaning they had learned, and would use it to represent a certain Japanese word whose meaning was usually similar to that of the Chinese character but which they had no way to write. This was a giant step forward, but they still faced two difficulties. One, Chinese was a monosyllabic language with no inflected words whereas Japanese was polysllabic with all those verb endings, particles, prefixes, and suffixes mentioned above. (With the passage of time this problem was solved by the invention of *kana.*)

The other problem was two-fold: the Japanese had difficulty pronouncing the Chinese readings perfectly (just as they have difficulty today with the pronunciation of English). That is, the Chinese reading of 林 was *lin,* but the Japanese could not say the *'l'* so they used *rin.* The second half of the problem was that Chinese pronunciation was not standard. Different dialects were spoken by the Chinese scholars who came to Japan to teach. Also, Chinese pronunciation changed somewhat—with the language reform edict of one or another emperor—over the 300 years that the Japanese were drinking deep of the Chinese cultural cup. (For a more detailed discussion of this process, see the chapter entitled "The Devil's Language?" in THE JAPANESE, Yohan Publications, Ltd., by this author.)

To give examples, the original Chinese reading of the character 山 for mountain was *shan,* but the Japanese version (i.e., the *on* reading) of that Chinese pronunciation was *san,* while the Japanese word for mountain was *yama.* Similarly, the original Chinese for the character 島 (island) was *dau* while the Japanese rendition (the *on*) was *tō* and the Japanese word itself was *shima.* 金 for metal was *chin,* which became *kin,* with the native word being *kane.*

When you come across a *kanji* in a two- or three-character compound, you are usually (but not quite always) safe in assuming that it should be pronounced in the *on* or Chinese manner. And when you find a *kanji* standing alone with several *kana* below it, like a tail, and maybe one above it, you should proceed on the assumption that it can be given its *kun* reading. Thus far, all fairly straightforward and reasonable, right?

But what if the *kanji* has more than one *on* reading, as some do? Which to use? Ah, here's the rub. The *kanji* 明 for "bright" has three *on* readings: *mei, myō,* and *min.* Say you discover it with the *kanji* 星 that has two *on* readings: *sei* and *jō* meaning "star."

Conceivably, this compound could have six possible pronunciations: *meisei, meijō, myōjō, myōsei, minjō,* and *minsei.*

The correct reading is *myōjō,* meaning the planet Venus (lit.,
bright star). Sadly, there is no rule or guide to tell the student which
to use. He must simply memorize it.

The Japanese child is spared this travail, for he is likely to know
the word *myōjō* for Venus before he meets its *kanji* and then can
readily fit the two together.

Or consider that dread *kanji* 生. It has two *on* readings, which
have the possible meanings of birth, life, subsistence, existence, and
student. Further, it has a long tedious list of *kun* readings with a
wide range of meanings: grassy place, genuine, crude, raw, breed,
happen, grow, arrange flowers (as in *ikebana*), and on and on, ad
nauseum.

Compounds containing 生 may sometimes have more than one
correct reading. For instance, 生業 may be read *seigyō, sugiwai,* or
nariwai (livelihood) while 生魚 may be pronounced *namazakana,
seigyo,* or *namauo.*

If the student is waiting for me to offer an easy solution to this
difficulty, he will have a long wait. I have none. I have read, however,
of a *kanji* dictionary being prepared by an Israeli named Jack
Halpern that should help with the problem of meaning, if not reading.
Reportedly, Mr. Halpern has given each *kanji* a "core meaning"—a
one-word meaning that the beginner should bear in mind over all the
others. This would be a valuable aid, and I look forward to being
able to review the book. I cannot envision how the compiler of this
dictionary, however, will decide what is the one-word core meaning
of a *kanji* like 坊 *(bō).* Note the various compounds of which this
character is a part:

nebō	oversleeping, a late-riser
akambō	a baby
bōzu	a Buddhist priest

Perhaps the compiler will take the most often used meaning and work from there. Still, the Naganuma *kanji* card for 坊 gives a "boy" and a "monk's living quarters attached to a temple" as the two basic meanings, and Nelson's Japanese-English Character Dictionary gives a "priest's residence" and a "boy" as basic meanings. If there is any connection between these two meanings, it is tenuous, and I would be hard pressed to know which to designate as the 'core meaning.' Be that as it may, I wish Mr. Halpern success.

The Shortest and Longest *Kanji*

一 is the character for one *(ichi)* and is obviously written with one stroke. 乙 *(otsu)* is also written with one stroke, but it takes some turns and twists. (*Otsu* means B. *Kō, otsu, hei* is the Japanese equivalent of A,B,C.)

The longest character in the dictionaries I have at hand is 龍龍龍 which is read *tō* or *dō* and means "dragons moving." I have never seen it in use, thank Buddha. Long ago, the abbreviated form 龍 came to be used and even that has been further abbreviated to 竜 with the *on* readings of *ryū* and *ryō* and the *kun* reading of *tatsu*. These mean just "dragon," not "dragons moving."

恐龍 or *kyōryū* (for dinosaur) employs this *kanji* as its second half. Literally, it means 'frightful dragon.'

The Number of *Kanji*

I have seen estimates of 80,000 as the number of *kanji* that have been used at one time or another in China and Japan. The best specific figure that I have is 40,543—the number given in the imperial Dictionary complied in 1710 by Chang-hsueh-shu and Chon-ting-ching.

But despair not. The Ministry of Education now recognizes only 1,945 *kanji* as the "daily use characters," although most college graduates will know about 3,000. 1,005 of the 1,945 are the *Kyōiku*

Kanji—those that should be learned during the nine years of compulsory education.

A Brief History

Kanji were born along the Yellow River in China, and a large number of them were already in use as far back as 1,200 B.C. They were brought to Japan by two Korean monks, Achiki and Wani. The king of Kudara in Korea had instructed them to carry three Chinese books to Japan: the CONFUCIAN ANALECTS, THOUSAND CHARACTER CLASSIC, and CLASSIC OF FILIAL PIETY. These gifts came during the reign of a Japanese emperor named Onin (270-312).

For almost 300 years thereafter, this imported written language was confined to the upper classes in Japan, but with the importation (and recognition in 540) of Buddhism, the knowledge of the *kanji* quickly became widespread. By the fifteenth century, Japanese and Chinese had become fused into a single language system.

During these many years, the *kanji* developed through stages from simple, if effective, pictograms to the standardized forms they are today:

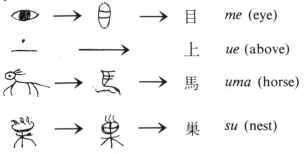

Our Approach to Learning *Kanji*

As noted earlier, I believe that most students will want to make some progress with the spoken language before beginning with the *kanji.* (You have already been shown the *kana,* and it is hoped that you are reviewing and using them daily). Now we will start introducing a small number of the most common *kanji* in each lesson, for both the sake of their utility and to give the student what I might call the 'philosophy of the *kanji.*' One or two or perhaps three compounds will be given with each character.

In college courses that weekly offer three hours of classroom instruction, it has been found that the student is able to learn 20 *kanji* every week. During my training in World War II, we must have learned 40 every week, for, in order to graduate, we had to pass tests verifying our knowledge of 2,600 characters. (This was before the blessed language reform in postwar Japan.) How fast, however, you progress must depend on your study time, circumstances, motivation, need, age, and linquistic talent.

Whatever pace you choose for yourself, I have some advice that should be helpful.

1. Use *kanji* cards.
2. Write each new character 100 times. If you will buy the squared paper the Japanese call *genkō yōshi,* you should use that for practice. (The squares come in several sizes.) This will also train you in the proper spacing and proportion.
3. Write the strokes of the *kanji* in their correct order.
4. You might use tracing paper to write over model characters. This should assist you in eventually writing well-balanced *kanji.*
5. Be especially careful to keep your vertical strokes perfectly straight. This is not easy, but the crooked vertical strokes (called *kugi-ori* or 'bent nail' strokes by the Japanese) are perhaps the most common failing in the calligraphy of foreigners.
6. If you are, like me, a *memo-ma* (a "memorandum demon" or dedicated note-taker), I suggest that you begin introducing an occasional *kanji* in those notes you take to jog your memory later. For example, you might jot down, "Ask wife how many friends to invite," but in lieu of "friends," you could write 友 *(tomo)* or, in place of "wife," you could pen, 愚妻 or *gusai* for 'my wife').

This will give you practice—and mystify your secretary. It will impress your casual acquaintances and arouse dark suspicions in the minds of your non-Japanese girl friends, or, for the fair sex, boy friends. (Keeps them on their toes, you know.) 頑張れ／*

 * *Gambare!* (Press on!)

Lesson Twelve

A.) Particles
B.) Conjunctions
C.) *To*—meaning if or when or with
D.) Phrases of location
E.) Interjections

Useful Everyday Expressions

Nan to iimasu ka. What is (this, that, it) called? [Lit., What do (you) say?]

Oboete imasu ka. Do you remember? (Lit., Are you remembering?)

Tsumaranai mono desu ga....
It is only a trifle (but)... (This is often said when handing someone a gift, no matter what its value.) See Cultural Sidelights.

Motto yukkuri itte kudasai.
Please say (it) more slowly. How we wore out this and the following sentence in our student days at the Japanese language school! Often we would have understood if only our *sensei* had spoken more slowly.

Mō ichido itte kudasai. Please say it once more.

O-tsukare-sama deshita.
You must be tired. (Honorific *o*—stem of verb *tsukareru*, to be tired—honorific *sama*, which is not always used as a title of address—past tense of copula *desu*) See Cultural Sidelights.

O-somatsu-sama deshita.
It was a poor meal. Said by the host or hostess in reply to *Go-chisō-sama deshita. Somatsu* is a Class B adjective meaning shabby, coarse, of poor quality. (Not always about food.)

Anō...
Pardon me... Well... Note the macron over the *o*. This is sometimes used like 'er' or 'uh' in English, but with an appropriate pause, it is often used to preface a request. See Cultural Sidelights.

155

Ano ne ...	Just a minute, please, or I say, there!	
Tabun sō deshō.	It is probably so.	

Vocabulary

yūbin-kyoku	post office		for him) and saying
nodo	throat		*Mottainai!* when
katachi	shape, form		you see someone
kaimono	shopping		wasting anything.
kata	shoulder	*kowai*	afraid,
daigaku	college,		frightening
	university	*tokkuri*	small ceramic flask
sakazuki	sake cup		in which *sake* is
kaminari	thunder		heated and served
chōchō	butterfly	*anaba*	a favorite bar (oft-
shūgi	tip (monetary)		en one off the
bangohan	evening meal		beaten path)
kippu uriba	ticket counter	*kōban* or	police substation,
kōshū denwa	public telephone	*kōbansho*)	also called a police
shashin-ya	photo studio		box
o-tenki	weather	*aite*	person with whom
toshokan	library		you do some-
kusuri-ya	pharmacy		thing, whether it be
takushii noriba	taxi stand		a sport, marriage,
o-tera	Buddhist temple		debate, drinking
mottainai	wasteful, too		bout, discussion, or
	good for. The		fight.
	dictionary de-	*tonde mo nai*	in early postwar
	finition given		days, G.I.s were ex-
	first, is, 'irrever-		cessively fond of
	ent, but I have		this expression,
	never heard it		which means 'out
	so used. Exam-		of the question' or
	ples of current		'absurd.' (A literal
	use are *Kare ni*		rendition would be,
	wa mottainai		'It won't even fly.')
	(It's too good		Nonetheless it is

standard Japanese
—but more polite-
ly put as *Tonde mo
arimasen.*

Pattern Sentences

(Bunkei)

1. *Jā, ikō yo. Hayaku ikanai to hi ga kureru.*   Say, let's go! If (we) don't go soon, it will be dark. (*Hi ga kureru*—the sun sets.)

2. *Teruko to kenka shita shi Midori ni okorareta kara yūutsu da.* I had a fight with Teruko, and Midori got mad at me so I'm really down in the dumps. (*Midori ni okorareru* literally means 'I was gotten mad at by Midori.' As a noun, *yūutsu* means melancholy. As a Class B adjective, *yūutsu* (*na*) means depressed, dejected, gloomy.)

3. *Are! Midori-chan ja nai ka! Konna kurai tokoro de nani shite iru nda?* I'll be...If it isn't Midori! Whatever are you doing in a dark place like this?

4. *Sakaya no tonari ni biriyādo no mise ga aru kara taihen benri desu.* There is a pool hall next door to the liquor store, so it's very convenient.

5. *Kora! Biiru wo suteru nante mottainai zo.* Hey! It's wasteful to do such a thing as throwing away beer. (Very rough in tone)

6. *Ara! Buchō-san desu no. Ureshii wa yo. Ē? Anaba e—? Yorokonde issho ni ikimasu tomo.* My! Is it the section chief? I'm so pleased to see you. What? To your favorite bar? Certainly I'll be happy to go with you. (*Tomo* carries the meaning of 'certainly.') Note that these words would be spoken by a woman.

7. *Sono hayashi no naka ni aru tatemono wa o-tera de sono ushiro ni mieru no wa daigaku desu.* The building amidst the woods is a Buddhist temple, and the one visible behind it is a university.

8. *Aokute kiiroi chōchō wa kōban no ue wo tonde imashita. Sō suru to, kaminari ga natte chōchō wa kowaku natte nigemashita.* A blue and yellow butterfly was flying over the police box. And when it thundered, the butterfly got scared and fled.

158

How to Use

Particles

In earlier lessons we took up certain particles or postpositions. Here we will take a closer look at some of them as well as considering new ones.

All such particles should be said without much emphasis and with almost no interval between them and the word they follow.

De denotes where an action takes place. *Nihon de horemashita.* I fell in love in Japan. It can show the means by which something is done. *Ashi de arukimasu.* I walk with (my) legs. It can tell the language used. *Kankoku-go de hanashimasu.* (I) speak in Korean. It can show scope. *Ichinen de ichiban atsui hi desu.* It is the hottest day of the year.

> *Terebi nyūsu de itte imashita ga...*(They) were saying on the *television* news that...

Mo is joined to *de* to form *de mo,* which usually means 'even.' *Onna de mo sensō de tatakaimasu.* (Even women fight in wars.) However, *de mo* can have the meaning of "or something." *Kōhī de mo motte kimashō ka.* Shall I bring coffee or something? Or it may be used to mean 'perhaps.' *Ginza ni de mo ikimashō ka.* Perhaps we should go to the Ginza?

Ni points to the location of animate and inanimate objects. *Uchi ni imasu.* I am at home. *Kikan-jū wa oshi-ire ni arimasu.* (My) machine gun is in the closet. Like *e, ni* can indicate direction. *Hawaii ni tobi-masu.* I will fly to Hawaii. *Ni* can tell the purpose of the action of the verb. *Ayamari ni ikimasu.* I will go to apologize. In the previous example, *ni* followed the stem of the verb *ayamaru,* but it can also be used in the same way after a noun. *Shokuji ni kimasu.* (He or she) is coming to dinner (actually, a meal.)

Ni before the verb *naru (narimasu)* for 'to become' tells what one becomes. *Gunjin ni narimasu.* I will become a soldier. *Ni* can mean 'for.' *Karada ni ii ndesu.* It is good for the body. It may or may not be used with *gozen* (morning) and *gogo* (afternoon). *Gogo deka-kemasu.* I will go out in the afternoon. *Gozen ni shite kurereba ariga-*

tai desu. If you do it in the morning, I will be grateful.— *Arigatai* is the adjective for grateful, of which *arigatō* is a form. *Nanji* (what time) is always followed by *ni* as in *Nanji ni shimashō ka.* What time shall I do it? The exception is when the *ni* is replaced by the particle *goro* (about). *Nanji goro shimashō ka.* About what time shall I do it?

Ni can mean both 'from' and 'to' in this slightly confusing instance: *Nihonjin no musume ni seppun wo naraimashita.* I learned how to kiss from a Japanese girl. *Nihonjin no musume ni seppun wo oshiemashita.* I taught (to) a Japanese girl how to kiss.

Uchi no jinan wa chōnan ni nite imasu. Our second son resembles our older son. In this instance, *ni* is used where there is no precise English equivalent. That is, 'to resemble (to) someone' is *dare ka ni nite iru* in Japanese.

Add *ni* to the dictionary form of a verb followed by the particle *no,* and we get 'in order to...' *Tegami wo kaku no ni kami to empitsu ga irimasu.* In order to write a letter, you need paper and pencil.

Consider the sentence *Daitōryo ni tegami wo kakimashita.* I wrote a letter to the president. Although it does not always follow, this shows the standard word order when *ni* comes after the indirect object: indirect object— *ni*—direct object— *wo*—verb.

Wo. We have already seen that the particle *wo* follows (and indicates) the direct object of a transitive verb. It is an anomaly of Japanese, however, that even certain intransitive verbs can take direct objects (followed by *wo*) as if they were transitive. Let us suppose that an action like flying, running, swimming, etc. takes place. Where that action is performed (such as the sky or a road or a river) is shown by the appropriate noun followed by *wo* (although we might have assumed that the particle would have been *de*). *Washi ga sora wo tonde imasu.* The eagle is flying in the sky. *Marason no senshu wa michi wo hashitte imasu.* The marathon runner is running along the road.

Itarō wa imōto wo nakasemashita. Itaro made his younger sister cry. *Naku* (to cry) is an intransitive verb and *nakaseru* is its causative form in the present tense. (*Nakaseta* or *nakasemashita* is the past tense.) In this example, the younger sister is the one who performs the action of the verb in its original form (*naku,* to cry), so *imōto* is followed by *wo,* then the causative form of the verb, e.g., *nakaseru.*

To: In addition to uses already presented, *to* can be used (like *ni*) in this phrase, *suihei to naru.* (to become a sailor). *To* is also used rather like quotation marks or 'that' before a speaker's words. *Okusan wa nan to iimashita ka.* (What did your wife say?) *Kao ni shiwa ga takusan aru kara hyaku-sai kurai da to omoimashita.* You have so many wrinkles on your face that I thought you were about 100-years-old.

Zutsu follows a number (or numerator) and means each, apiece, or at a time, *Ato de shokupan to raimugipan wo hitotsu zutsu katte kimasu.* Later I will go out to buy one loaf each of white bread and dark bread. *Minna wa sono kojiki ni issen-en zutsu agemashita.* Everyone gave that beggar ¥1,000 each.

Conjunctions

Lesson Seven demonstrated uses of the conjunctions meaning 'and:' *to, ya,* and *sō shite.* There is, however, another of which you should be aware: *shi.*

Shachō wa karada no guai ga warui shi okusan ni mo nigeraremashita. (The president is in ill health, and his wife has run off on him.) Two points to note: Here, *shi* follows an adjective, which is common. Also, the passive voice of the verb *nigeru* (to run off) is used to express the flight of the wife.

In addition, there are other words or phrases of conjunctive force that you should remember: We have already met some of them, but they are listed here again for your review:

sore ni	and	*sono ue*	on top of
mata	and	*oyobi*	and
soko de	and	*sō shitara*	and
de wa	so	*sō suru to*	and
sore tomo	or	*narabi ni*	and

aruiwa	or	*sore de*	therefore
ga	but	*sore de wa*	(on starting a new topic)

When two adjectives of the A Class are used together, the *kute* form of the first adjective serves as a conjunction.

ōkikute akai   big and red

If the first adjective is of the B Class, then *de* is used, since this kind of adjective does not conjugate.

kirei de shinsetsu   pretty and kind

O-sake mo nomu shi yo-asobi mo shimasu. (He, she) drinks *sake* and goes out pleasure-seeking at night.

De, which is actually the stem of the copula *desu* (or *deshita*), can be used conjunctively:

Waifu wa nijū-go-sai de musuko wa kokonotsu desu. My wife is 25-years-old, and my son is nine.

To—meaning if or when or with

We have seen that the particle *to* can be used as a conjunction, as in *otōsan to sono musuko* (a father and his son.).

It can also be used to mean 'with,' as in *Watakushi to itte kureru hito wa imasen ka.* Who will go with me? (Lit., Me—with—condescending to go person—is there not?)

Or it can mean 'against,' as in *Yūwaku to tatakau*–to struggle against temptation.

Still another common and handy use of *to* is after a subordinate clause to mean 'if' or 'when':

Kanojo ni denwa wo kakeru to, kanojo no otōsan ga demashita. When I telephoned her, her father answered.

Hi ga deru to atatakaku narimasu. When the sun comes up, it gets warm.

In the above usage, *to* usually follows the dictionary form of the verb, e.g. *tatakau, agaru, deru, kuru, iu, hanasu,* et al. Sometimes, however, it may be used after a polite form of the verb, that is, the verb stem with *-masu: Nihon ni ikimasu to*—or When (you) go to Japan—

To may be used after the present tense of the verb (whether polite or informal) in a subordinate clause even though that sentence's final verb may be in the past tense. For instance, *Sakuban okusan ni michi de au to kanojo wa naite imashita. Dō shimashita ka.* When I met your wife on the street last night, she was crying. What happened? As you can see, the tense of the final verb *naku* governs the tense of the subordinate clause verb *au.*

Phrases of Location

You have been introduced to a number of nouns that show location, such as *uchi* for inside, *ue* for above, *saki* for beyond, and so forth.

Often these become the central word in what are called phrases of location. The central noun is preceded by *no* and followed by *ni, e,* or *de.*

An example is *Yama no mukō ni nani ga arimasu ka* or What is beyond the mountain(s)?

(Lit., Mountain(s)—of—beyond—in—what—as for—is?)

Another: *Bengoshi no uchi de kenka wo shite kimashita.* I had a fight (lit., came fighting) at the lawyer's house.

From these examples you can see that a noun or personal pronoun precedes the initial *no* in the phrase of location to define what location we are discussing. Also, it is possible to use one of the *ko, so, a,* or *do* adjectival pronouns in place of the noun or personal pronoun. When you use one of these, however, the initial *no* is incorporated in the adjectival pronoun: *ko(no,) so(no), a(no),* or *do (no). Sono ura e ikimasu ka.* Are you going behind there?

The central noun of the phrase of location is followed by *ni, de,* or *e.* Which of these three to choose is determined by the verb. *De* is used when the following verb is one of action: *Gakkō no shokudō de tabemashita.* I ate in the school's dining room. *Ni* is used when the verb indicates the static location of something. *Akai jitensha wa uchi no yoko ni arimasu.* A red bicycle is beside our house. *E* is used to indicate destination or direction with a verb of motion. *Tarō wa kaji no hō e hashitte ikimashita.* Taro ran toward the fire. (Lit. Taro —as for—fire's—direction—toward—running—went.)

Here are more phrases of location:

no mawari ni, de, e	around
no uchi ni, de, e	within
no saki ni, de, e	beyond, at the head of
no omote ni, de, e	in front of
no naka ni, de, e	within
no shita ni, de, e	under
no soba ni, de, e	beside
no soto ni, de, e	outside
no tonari ni, de, e	next door
no temae ni, de, e	this side of
no ura ni, de, e	in back of
no ushiro ni, de, e	behind
no chikaku ni, de, e	vicinity
no mae ni, de, e	before

Interjections

As in English, Japanese interjections are used to express surprise, shock, doubt, anger, pain, fear, interest, encouragement, and an invitation to agreement.

Generally, they can be divided into interjections that stand alone or precede the phrase or sentence—and those that come at the end of sentences.

Among those that stand alone or precede the sentence are the following. Note that the English translations that accompany them are sometimes only approximations, there being no precise English equivalents.

aita	ouch	*mā*	my
kore	here now	*sore, sora*	there
kora	hey (rough)	*sā*	well; come
ā	ah	*chotto*	just a minute
ne	I say. Don't you think so?	*nani!*	hmph!
		ō	oh
oya	oh	*ara*	my goodness (feminine)
dore	what	*yō*	hullo (masculine)
are	hark, look	*jā* (or *de wa*)	well
ē?	what? well?		

Interjections coming at the end of the sentence or phrase include such as:

Zo emphasizes what was said. It is rough and masculine. *Atsui zo.* (It's really hot.)   Used only among very close male friends.

Ze is used in the same way as *zo* above.

Ne or *nē* invites agreement, as in *Ikimashō, ne?* Let's go, shall we? The speaker assumes that his auditor shares his viewpoint.

No is sometimes used by women in place of the interrogative *ka*, as in, *Konya doko de nemasu no.* Where will you sleep tonight?

Men sometimes used *nā* instead of *ne*. *Sono jiko wa hidokatta nā.* That accident was terrible, wasn't it?

After the dictionary form of a verb, *na* becomes a negative imperative. *Shinjuku no bā ni iku na.* Don't go to Shinjuku bars.

Tomo after a sentence carries the meaning of 'certainly!' *Agemasu tomo.* Certainly I'll give it (to you).

The feminine *wa* is also emphatic at the end of a sentence. *Kono akachan wa kawaii wa.* (How cute this baby is!)

The *a* vowel in *sā* at the beginning of a sentence is long, but at the end of a sentence or word the vowel is short. Here *sa* is used for emphasis. *Sore wa atarimae sa.* (Surely that's obvious.)

The interrogative interjection (or particle) *ka* and the emphatic *yo* have already been discussed.

Cultural sidelights:

*** *O-tsukare-sama deshita* is often used to show that you appreciate someone's hardwork or difficulty. Employees may say these words to others leaving at the end of the day. If she is a friendly sort, a wife may say them to her husband when he returns from the office. Correct usage, however, would not permit her to so express herself when he comes home later from carousing in bars, for the expression is meant to shows appreciative awareness of hard work, not hard play. The loud speakers used in transportation systems can be heard tirelessly assuaging the passengers' feelings with this expression, for getting around in Japan has always been a chore—although less so nowadays. *Ryokan* employees will also chant this to newly-arrived guests who, it is assumed, have just disembarked from wearisome train or bus journeys.

*** It is proper to demonstrate hesitation and reserve when making a request or when addressing a superior on any matter. To plunge right away into the heart of the matter is the antithesis of good manners. *Anō* followed by a pause—perhaps with head bowed—suggests that you are overwhelmed with awe and stunned at your own presumption in addressing such an obviously superior being. (The customary reply to *Anō...* is *Hai, nan deshō ka.* Yes, what is it?)

*** Saying *Tsumaranai mono desu ga dōzo...* when handing someone a gift is proper etiquette, but good manners do not end there. The way it is given is equally important. If you give someone a magazine, for example, it should be positioned so that the recipient can readily read the front cover. This applies to *meishi* or business cards as well. I recall one foreign businessman who went to the trouble of having business cards made before coming to Japan but thereafter ruined this potentially favorable impression by passing them out at the conference table as if casually dealing from a deck of cards. The ultimate in etiquette requires that both hands be used in offering the present or, if it is very small, that it be handed over in one hand with the other hand hovering in the air nearby, ready to offer further service. In any case, never just sit on your empty hand.

And, of course, the proffering of the present should be done with an obeisance, the depth of which is determined by the relationship and the occasion. Don't just stand there like a stick and casually hand over the offering, no matter how flowery the polite words are that you send along in accompaniment.

Finally, when you are the recipient, you should consider the packing or wrappings in which the gift is contained. Some wrappings are obviously intended to go along with the gift permanently, but others may not be. When I had been in Japan only a year and was about to return home at the end of my first tour of duty, the inn-keeper of the *ryokan* we had sequestered as our officers' billet brought me a parting gift. It was a lacquered box wrapped in a beautiful silk *furoshiki*. I expressed my admiration for both items extravagently, replaced the box within the silk wrapping cloth and put the bundle on the *tatami* behind me. It took the poor inn-keeper five or so minutes to bring himself to indicate to me that he wanted the *furoshiki* returned.

Kanji

We will now begin introducing a number of *kanji* and typical compounds *(jukugo)* in each lesson.

The *kanji* itself is given first, then the *on* reading(s), *kun* reading (s), meaning(s), direction of strokes, order of strokes, and one to three compounds with their readings and meanings.

As we advance in the course, the order and direction of the character strokes will be omitted, since the student should become habituated to them before long. (Remember the rule: vertical strokes are drawn from top to bottom, horizontal strokes from left to right.)

An effort has been made to make everything about the *kanji* as simple and basic as possible at this stage. Some textbooks load the student down with footnotes, supplemental readings, not-so-common compounds, etc, but here we strive to familiarize the student with a basic meaning or two, teach him how to write the character, and expose him to only one or two (no more than three) of the most useful compounds. To be sure, there is more to be learned about

Kanji	On reading(s)	Kun reading(s)	Meaning(s)	Stroke direction	Stroke order	Compounds (jukugo) In Kanji	Reading(s)	Meaning(s)
一	ichi	hito(tsu)	one	一→	一 1	一番	ichiban	first
二	ni	futa(tsu)	two	二	二 1 2	二人	futari	numerator for two people
三	san	mit(tsu)	three	三	三 1 2 3	三日	mikka	3 days or 3rd day of month
日	nichi, jitsu	hi	day, sun	目	日 1 2 3 4	一日	ichinichi	one day
							tsuitachi	first day of month
						毎日	mainichi	everyday
						今日	kyō konnichi→	today (more formal)
月	getsu, gatsu	tsuki	month, moon	月	月 1 2	月曜日	getsuyōbi	Monday
						二ヶ月	nikagetsu	two months
						二月	nigatsu	February
							futatsuki	two months
水	sui	mizu	water	氷	水 1 2 3 4	水曜日	suiyōbi	Wednesday
						水分	suibun	moisture, water content
土	do, to	tsuchi	soil	土	土 1 2 3	土地	tochi	land
						土曜日	doyōbi	Saturday
四	shi, yo or yon	yot(tsu)	four	四	四 1 2 3 4 5	四月	shigatsu	April
						四日	yokka	four days
								4th day of month
五	go	itsu(tsu)	five	五	五 1 2 3 4	五日	itsuka	five days 5th day of month
上	jō	ue. a(geru) aga(ru)	above, give, rise	上	上 1 2 3	上手	jōzu	skillful
						上下	jōge	up and down

these *kanji,* but for the present too much detail would be counter-productive.

When parentheses are used in the *kun* reading(s), they mean that the syllable or syllables inside the parentheses are added to the *kanji* as *kana.* For instance, this is the *kanji* for eight: 八. The *on* reading of 八 is *hachi,* but if we append つ *(tsu)* to 八, we read it in the *kun* manner, or *yat(tsu).* In Japanese, of course, it appears as 八つ.

In fortunate cases, a *kanji* will have just one basic meaning, although there will be differing *kun* and *on* readings. In other cases, the *on* may have one meaning and the *kun* another. If such instances were few and clear-cut, we would list the meanings of the *on* and the *kun* separately so there would be no problem. All too often, however, we are confronted with a *kanji* like 月 (see below). The *on* readings are *getsu* and *gatsu,* while the *kun* is *tsuki. Getsu* and *gatsu* usually refer to month, an exception being *getsuyōbi* (Monday or 'Moonday'). Then, if *tsuki* meant only moon, we could separate the two. Sadly, *tsuki* can mean both moon and month, although *getsu* or *gatsu* can mean only month (except in the above case of *getsuyōbi*).

The solution? There is none. Just memorize each different usage. That's what 120 million Japanese (plus a few foreigners) have done, and you too can do it.

Lesson Thirteen

A.) *bakari*
B.) *-kata*
C.) *yō*
D.) *oku*
E.) *miru, -te (-de) miru*
F.) *-yasui* and *-nikui*
G.) *-sō desu*

Useful Everyday Expressions

Yōkoso irasshaimashita.   Welcome.
  (*Yoku* may be used, but
   yōkoso is slightly
    more emphatic.)
O-sumai wa dochira desu ka.
                    Where is your home?
Mae ni o-me ni kakarimashita.
                    I have met you before. (Lit., Before...honorable
                    eyes...in...have hung.)

Odoroita!   What a surprise! (Lit., I was surprised.)
Tanomu kara...   Please do it for me. This is said at the conclu-
                    sion of a request to someone with whom you
                    are intimate, but not, for example, to your
                    section chief at the office.

Dōzo o-saki ni... Please go ahead of me. (When we boarded a
                    train for Osaka just after our arrival in Japan
                    long ago, my classmates and I took punning
                    delight in saying to each other: *Dōzo Ōsaka
                    ni....*)

O-saki ni, dōmo... Thanks for letting me go ahead.
Usotsuke!   Says you! Don't talk rot! (Lit., Lie!)
O-negai da kara... Please, I'm begging you... This is like *Tanomu
                    kara...* above, except that it can precede the
                    request as well as follow it.

O-tesū desu ga... I'm sorry to bother you (but)... (lit., Honorable
                    —hands—many—are—but...)

169

Vocabulary

noru	to ride	*shijin*	poet
yowai	weak	*yopparai*	drunkard,
wataru	to cross, as		boozer
	a street or	*yakusu*	to translate
	sea	*yaoya*	green grocer
kumoru	to become	*erabu*	to choose, select
	cloudy	*tsumetai*	chilly (as a wind); cold
kuruma	cart; also often		(as a drink… or heart)
	used to mean	*tsuzukeru*	to continue (human)
	auto	*ke*	hair; (animal) fur
nureru	to be or become	*tsukeru*	to attach to, to turn on
	wet		(as a light); to charge
genkan	entrance-way		an expense
shikaru	to scold	*yūgata*	evening
setsumei	explanation	*yobu*	to call
yomu	to read	*yōji*	business; something
sore nara	if so…		that needs to be done
matsu	to wait for	*yorokobu*	to rejoice, to be glad
depāto	department store	*kōjō*	factory
motsu	to have, to hold	*nakanaka* *	very (as in a very
hankachi	handkerchief		pretty girl)

*Other uses: *Kanai wa nakanaka kaerimasen.* My wife is very late in returning.
Sono Furansu-jin wa nakanaka no shijin desu. That Frenchman is quite a poet.

Pattern Sentences
(Bunkei)

1. *Kono jā-jā-buri wa yūgata made ni yami-sō mo nai desu.* This heavy rain does not look as if it will end by evening. (*jā-jā-buri*—lit., noisy fall—means a heavy rain. *Dosha-buri*—lit., earth and gravel fall—is a similar expression analogous to 'raining cats and dogs'.)

2. *Soto wa samuku-nasasō desu.* It does not seem to be cold outside. (The final *i* in *samuku-nai* has been dropped and replaced be *-sasō.*)

3. *Ureshisō desu, ne.* You seem happy.

4. *Kongetsu hajimari-sō desu.* It will probably begin this month.

5. *Dekiru yō nara yatte mite kudasai.* If it seems that you can, go ahead and try it.

6. *Atete mimasu.* I will try to guess. (*Ateru*=to guess)

7. *Mō kaetta sō desu.* I am told (he) has already gone home.

8. *Kono goro kumotte bakari imasu.* It's always cloudy these days.

9. *Kanojo wa utsukushii bakari de nan no yaku ni mo tachimasen.* She is just beautiful but is of no use whatsoever. (*Yaku ni tatsu*=to be useful)

10. *Kisha wa shuppatsu suru bakari ni natte imasu.* The train is on the point of leaving. (*Shuppatsu suru*=to depart)

11. *Tonari no uchi ni sunde iru no wa Fuirippin-jin bakari desu.* Only Filipinos live in the house next door.

12. *Senshu no erabi-kata wa fukōhei desu.* (That) way of choosing the players is not fair. (*Fukōhei*= unfair)

13. *Sensei wa komban uchi ni kuru yō na koto wo osshaimashita.* The teacher said (he/she) would come to my home tonight.

14. *Sono yō na hanashi wa yoku kiku ga ikkō ni shinjimasen.* I often hear that kind of story but don't believe it at all.

15. *Iki wo shite iru to iu bakari desu.* All I can say is I am still alive.

16. *Sakimura-san no namae wa kiita bakari de shaku ni sawaru.* Just hearing Mr. Sakimura's name is enough to make me mad. (Either *wa* or *wo* after *namae* would be correct.)

17. *Kanai wa kyōdai no mae ni bakari suwatte keshō wo shimasu.* My wife does nothing but sit in front of the dressing table and put on make-up.

18. *Depāto ni wa kono yō na hankachi wa arimasen deshita.* There were no handkerchiefs like this in the department store.

19. *Sannan ni shako no dentō wo tsukeru yō ni ii-nasai.* Tell our (third) son to turn on the garage light.

20. *Sono yō na setsumei wa shinji-nikui desu.* That kind of explanation is hard to swallow (believe).

21. *Anata wa kaimono bakari shite iru kara komarimasu yo.* All you do is shop, and this troubles me.

22. *Hataraite bakari ite zenzen asobanai to Jakku wa tsumaranai ningen ni narimasu.* All work and no play makes Jack a dull person.

23. *Nan no yō da. Mata kane ka. Kinō gosen-en yatta bakari ja nai ka.* What do you want? More money? I just gave you five thousand yen yesterday, you know.

24. *Shiranai bakari de naku shiritaku mo arimasen.* I don't only do not know; I don't even want to know.

25. *Areppakari no ke nara tokoya ni iku riyū wa sukoshi mo arimasen.* With only that amount of hair, there's not the slightest reason to go to the barber shop (*Areppakari= are bakari*).

26. *Hikōki ni wa jūnin bakari notte imashita.* Only ten people were aboard the plane.

27. *Sanjikan bakari matte kara okotte uchi ni kaerimashita.* After waiting about three hours, I became angry and returned home.

28. *Sono inago no tsukudani wa amari oishi-sō de wa arimasen.* Those locusts boiled in soy sauce do not look to be very appetizing.

How to Use

Bakari

When we first encountered *bakari* in language school, we were told that it meant 'only,' which was, I think, the only meaning I, for one, knew for the word for quite a while after that. With age, however, came wisdom, and in the richness of time, I became aware of other meanings in frequent use.

Anyway, *bakari* is used after—always *after*—nouns, gerunds, adjectives, (some) particles and present and past tenses of verbs, as we will see in a moment. After nouns, *bakari* may be followed by certain particles, as suggested, but not all. Even though grammatical logic would suggest that *ga* or *wo* or *mo* should succeed *bakari* in consideration of its function, it is better not to inject any of these three.

For instance, in addition to 'only,' *bakari* may relay such connotations as about, be on the verge of, have no choice but, keep on doing, do nothing but, nearly, and mere.

Although its various divergent meanings may vex the soul of the ardent student, it is nonetheless a most useful and frequently met word. Engrave it on your liver; *bakari* will serve you well in the future.

Example: *Imo-jōchū bakari nomu to me ga mienaku narimasu yo.* If you drink only home brew, you will go blind. (*Imo-jōchū* is a kind of unrefined sake drunk mostly in rural settings.) See pattern sentences for more examples of how to use *bakari* as well as the·constructions introduced below.

-kata

-kata means manner or method. When attached to the stem of a verb, it has the meaning of 'how to.'

Uma no norikata wa shiranai yō desu, ne. It seems you don't know how to ride a horse, do you?

yō

Yō is another valuable word with several meanings, chief among them being method, like, kind, appearance, and seems as if.

Like *-kata* above, it is attached to the stem of a verb to mean how something is done: *yobi-yō*=how to call, *oyogi-yō*=how to swim, *kangae-yō*=how to think (or how one thinks).

Shimbun wo yomu to raishū sensō ga okoru yō desu. If you read the newspaper, it looks as if war will break out (happen) next week.

Oku

Alone, the verb *oku* means to place or to put, but when it follows a gerund, it has the meaning of 'to do' (the action of the gerund) for future reference or use. That is to say, there is a lapse of time between the action expressed in the gerund and the time when that action will be of use. Whereas *gohan wo taku* would mean to boil rice for use now, *gohan wo taite oku* would mean to boil rice now to eat later. Or, *Taishi no enzetsu wo yakushite okimasu.* I will translate the ambassador's speech now (so that the translation will be available later, when needed.)

Miru

In addition to 'see' and 'look,' *miru*—when used after a gerund—means to try.

Kono tsumetai biiru wo nonde mite kudasai. Try this cold beer. (This does not mean to see if you can drink it but to drink it and see how it tastes.)

-yasui and *-nikui*

As suffixes, *-nikui* means hard, while *-yasui* means easy. They are attached to the stem of a verb. *Yomi-yasui* is easy to read and *yomi-nikui* is hard to read. *Wakari-nikui* is difficult to understand, and *wakari-yasui* is simple of comprehension.

Sō desu (sō da)

After the present or past tense of a verb, *sō desu* means 'I hear that,' 'it is said that,' 'the story goes that,' etc.

Ashita wa kumoru sō desu. (They) say it will be cloudy tomorrow.

Sometimes *sō desu* (or—more plainly—*sō da*) is attached to the stem of a verb or adjective to introduce the meaning of probability or appearance.

Yuki ga furi-sō desu. It looks as if it will snow.

Sō attached to the stem of a verb and followed by *na* and then a noun gives the meaning of 'about to.' *Naki-sō na kao,* for example, would be a face about to cry. *Tobi-sō na kotori* would be a bird about to fly. *Nige-sō na neko* would be a cat about to flee.

After *sō* on the stem of a verb or adjective, we can use such negative constructions as *de nai, de wa nai, ja nai, de wa arimasen, mo nai,* and *mo arimasen. Sono yopparai wa tachi-sō de wa arimasen.* It does not look as if that drunkard will stand up.

Cultural sidelights:

*** *Yōkoso (yoku) irasshaimashita* is said to welcome guests to your home, but care should be taken not to confuse this expression with *irasshai* (or the somewhat more polite *irasshai-mase*).

When you enter a shop or restaurant, those who will serve you often mark your entry with cries of *Irasshai! Irasshai!* (The louder the cries, the lower the level of decorum and class.)

Fishmongers are notorious in this regard. In fact, in the open-air fish shops, the untutored may wonder in alarm if the mongers are not about to set upon the customers in an inexplicable rage.

Anyway, uttering *Irasshai* is the custom, and you need not say anything in reply. In fact, to respond with *Konnichi wa* or any greeting would be thought eccentric or even *outrè*.

Sometimes, however, especially among women who foregather often, we hear a casual *Irasshai* in lieu of *Yoku irasshaimashita*.

*** *Bakari* is only one of many Japanese words meaning 'about.' Among others that *precede* the word described are such as: *yaku, daitai, oyoso* (or *ōyoso*),*hobo,* and *zatto.*

> *Shōsetsu wa hobo kansei shimashita.* The novel is almost finished.
>
> *Oyoso atatte imasu.* That's about right.
>
> *Zatto hyaku-dai no kuruma.* About 100 cars.

Among those that *follow* the word described are *kurai (gurai), hodo, bakari,* and *koro* or *goro* in regards to time.

This reflects hesitation to express exact numbers. In Japan, you may have the experience of hearing a customer telling the man at the local *yaoya* that she wants "about three" *daikon* (radish), even though it is likely that she knows exactly how many she needs. One reason that many Japanese avoid such preciseness is the belief that it smacks of a display of superior knowledge. Another is consideration for others. That is, they like to give the other fellow some leeway in choosing how he will respond.

Study recommendations:

Some learners like to set aside a certain time daily for study, then largely ignore such efforts the rest of the time.

But, as noted in a book called A FOREIGN LANGUAGE AND I, your studies should be "continuous and passionate." By all means, study two hours after dinner every evening or whatever, but don't stop there. Use every available moment to practice and review. Listen closely to the conversation of Japanese near you. Try to read *kanji* signs on the street and jot down unknown *kanji* to look up later. Place dictionaries by your TV set and refer to them often. Always ask the meanings of words you don't understand.

As the book says, pursue your studies with passion. Burn the midnight oil. The Japanese say, *Keisetsu no kō wo tsumu,* which means something like: Pile up the benefits that accrue from studying by the light of fireflies reflected on the snow.

Kanji	On reading(s)	Kun reading(s)	Meaning(s)	Stroke direction	Stroke order	Compounds (jukugo) In Kanji	Reading(s)	Meaning(s)
木	moku	ki	tree			木曜日	mokuyōbi	Thursday
金	kin	kane	metal, money, gold			金持ち	kanemochi	rich person
						税金	zeikin	tax
						金曜日	kinyōbi	Friday
山	san	yama	mountain			沢山	takusan	much, many
						火山	kazan	volcano
川	sen	kawa	river					
本	hon	moto	book, base			本当 (な)	hontō (na)	true
人	jin. nin	hito	person			日本人	Nihonjin	Japanese
						主人	shujin	husband
						外人	gaijin	foreigner
火	ka	hi	fire			火曜日	kayōbi	Tuesday
六	roku	mut(tsu)	six			六日	muika	six days
								sixth day of month
						六人	rokunin	six persons
七	shichi	nana(tsu)	seven			七日	nanoka	seven days
								seventh day of month
						七時	shichi-ji	seven o'clock
下	ge, ka	shita	under			下さい	kudasai	please (give, do)
		sa(garu)	to hang down			下着	shitagi	underwear

Lesson Fourteen

A.) *Koto*
1. *koto ga dekiru*
2. *koto ga aru (nai)*
3. *koto ni suru (naru)*
4. *koto desu (da)*
5. *(samui) koto wa (samui)*
6. *koto, to no koto, to iu koto*
7. *koto*

B.) (conditional verb) *to suru* or *to omou*

C.) *kamo shiremasen*

D.) *-shidai*

Useful Everyday Expressions

(Okusan) ni yoroshiku.	My regards to your (wife).
Dame desu! (da!)	That's out of the question (!)
	That's no good (!)
Nani wo nasaimashita ka.	What did you do? (very polite)
Yasumimashō.	Let's take a break. Or, Let's go to bed.
Goran kudasai.	Look.
O-kinodoku desu.	I'm sorry to hear that. (Lit., It must be poison to your honorable spirit.)
Mōshiwake arimasen.	I have no excuse. I am sorry.
Dō shimashita ka.	What's the matter?
O-matase shimashita.	I'm sorry to keep you waiting.
O-daiji ni.	Take care.
Mata, dōzo.	Please come again.
Suteki desu, ne.	That's fine. How wonderful! It's just great. May be used (mostly by women) about almost anything you admire: a party, dinner, beauty, outfit.
Keiki wa dō desu ka. Mā, botsu-botsu desu.	How's business? Well, just so-so.
Warui kedo, tanomu yo.	Said (informally) after you have asked a favor of someone. (Lit., bad . . . however. . . I ask it!)

(Sūgaku) no benkyō de tsukaremashita.   (I) am tired from studying mathematics.

(Watakushi wa) mon-nashi desu.   (I) am flat broke.

(Miso-shiru) wo meshi-agarimasu ka.   Will you have some (soy soup)?

Vocabulary

shio	salt	*yakyū*	baseball
noboru	to climb	*yasumu*	to take a rest, also, to go to bed at night
fukai	deep		
miru	to look, see	*chikara*	strength, power
tamago	egg	*teinei (na)*	polite; also, careful
magaru	to bend, turn	*yaseru*	to become or to be thin
shikaru	to scold	*harau*	to pay
chūi	attention	*nugu*	to take off, as a hat or clothing
taisetsu (na)	important		
te	hand	*kembutsu*	sight-seeing
toru	to take	*morau*	to receive
ni tsuite	concerning (follows nouns)	*hazukashii*	embarrassing, shy
		rekishi	history
riyū	reason	*hajimaru*	to begin (v.i.)
hairu	to enter	*hajimeru*	to begin (v.t.)
shiraseru	to inform, let know		

Pattern Sentences

(Bunkei)

1. *Kanojo ni wa hazukashii riyū ga aru no ka mo shirenai desu.*
   She may have an embarrassing reason (for not doing something.)
2. *Shiken ni ochita no wa jūbun benkyō shinakatta kara desu.*
   Failing the test is due to not studying enough.
   (*Shiken ni ochiru*=to fail a test. Lit., to fall in a test.)
3. *Ginza no Suehiro de maiban bifuteki wo taberu koto ni shimasu.*
   I make it a habit of having a beefsteak at Suehiro's on the Ginza every evening. (Suehiro is a famous steakhouse.)

4. *Minna de sono bā no takai kanjō wo harau koto ni shimashita.*
    We decided we would all (contribute to) pay that bar's expensive
    bill.
5. *Yakyū wo mi ni ikō to omottara sensei ni Nihongo wo benkyō suru
    yō ni iwaremashita.*   I planned to go watch baseball, but the teacher
    told me to study Japanese.
6. *Hantoshi bakari de Nihongo wo narau koto wa dekimasen.*
    It is impossible to learn Japanese in only half a year.
7. *Hitori de kurashite iru node sabishii ka mo shiremasen.*
    Because (he, she) is living alone, (he, she) may be lonely.
8. *Nan no koto desu ka.*   What are you talking about?
    (Lit., What thing is it?)
9. *Mishigan-daigaku no gakusei-tachi wa raishū Kyōto wo kembutsu
    suru to no koto desu.*   I hear that the students from the University
    of Michigan will go sightseeing in Kyoto next week.
10. *Gohan mo shokupan mo tabenakereba yaseru ka mo wakarimasen.*
    If you eat neither rice nor bread, you may lose weight.
    (While *pan* is a basic word for bread, you will likely hear *shoku-
    pan* more often. *Shoku-pan* literally means 'eating bread:' one
    wonders what other kind there is or why it is necessary to make
    the distinction.)
11. *Sono shigoto wa sonna ni teinei ni suru koto wa nai no desu.*
    It is not necessary to do that work so carefully.
12. *Kōchō-sensei no jijo wa Shimbashi de tokidoki yoru osoku made
    asobu koto mo arimasu.*
    The (school) principal's second daughter sometimes goes to Shimba-
    shi for night-time amusements.
13. *Anzen da yo. Nani mo chūi suru koto wa arimasen.*
    It's safe! There is nothing to be careful about (to watch out for).
14. *Butai de Koshi Keiko-san wa yōfuku wo zembu nuida ga ato de kei-
    satsu ni shikararemashita.*
    Miss Keiko Koshi took off all her clothes on the stage, but she was
    scolded later by the police.

How to Use
Koto

Koto is a word of multifarious uses and meanings, such as fact,
event, cause, experience, matter, and circumstances.

1. *Koto ga dekiru.* (This matter—as for—can be done.) The dictionary form of a verb followed by *koto ga dekiru* lends a potential meaning. (The particle after *koto* is always *ga,* never *wa.*)

Aruku koto ga dekimasu.	(I) can walk.
Hanasu koto ga dekimasu.	(I) can speak.
Dasu koto ga dekimasu.	(I) can take (it) out or put (it) out.

See the pattern sentences for more examples of this construction as well as the others given below.

2. *Koto wa (ga) aru; koto wa (ga) nai.* There is such a thing as . . .; there is not such a thing as . . . *Kanojo ni hanashita koto wa arimasen.* I have never spoken to her. *Doyōbi ni eiga wo mi ni iku koto wa arimasu.* I sometimes go to see a movie on Saturday. (Or, There is such a thing as my seeing a movie on Saturday.)

3. *Koto ni suru.* I (or other pronoun) decided to . . . *Kagoshima ni asobi ni iku koto ni shimashita.* (I) decided to go to Kagoshima for pleasure.

    Koto ni naru. It was decided that. . . (a decision made by someone other than the person speaking). *Kagoshima ni asobi ni iku koto ni narimashita.* It was decided that (we) would go to Kagoshima for pleasure.

    The verb before *koto* in both forms may, of course, be negative: *Kagoshima ni ikanai koto ni shimashō.* Let's decide against going to Kagoshima.

    Koto ni suru also can convey the message of being in the habit of doing something or making it a point to do something. *Maiasa umi de oyogu koto ni shimasu.* I make it a rule to swim in the ocean every morning.

4. *Koto desu (da). Ojiisan no koto da ga...*
    It is about grandfather (but)...

5. (Verb or adjective) *koto wa* (same verb or adjective). Using the same verb or adjective both before and after *koto wa* fortifies the truth of the statement. *Sabishii koto wa sabishii*

ndesu. I am, to be sure, lonely. *Fuji-san wo nobotta koto wa nobotta desu ga...* Yes, I did indeed climb Mt. Fuji (but)...

6. *koto.* The dictionary form of a verb, e.g., the infinitive (*nugu*=to take off), can be used as the subject of a sentence when followed by *koto. Kyabarē ni hairu koto wa tada desu.* To enter the cabaret is free. Remember that *koto* can be replaced by '*no.*' *Kyabarē ni hairu no wa tada desu.* Same meaning.

To no koto and *to iu koto* both mean 'It is said that . . .' The latter is often heard in news broadcasts. *Rainen no fuyu wa motto atatakai to no koto desu.* It is said that next winter will be warmer. *Fukuoka no shichō wa myōnichi Guamu-tō ni tatsu to iu koto desu.* It is reported that the mayor of Fukuoka will leave for Guam tomorrow. (*-tō* after '*Guamu*' means island.)

7. *koto.* After a word or sentence, *koto* has the force of a feminine exclamation mark:

Hana no utsukushii koto! How lovely the flowers are!

Osoi koto! How slow (or late) (he) is!

Tenki no ii koto! What fine weather it is!

Koto has a seemingly endless variety of other idiomatic uses:

koto ni yoru to . . .	depending on how things develop . . .
koto naku sumu	to proceed without any problems (lit., to end without a 'thing')
koto-nakare shugi	principle of peace at any price (lit., be there not a thing principle)
koto ni yotte wa	if need be (lit., depending on things)

(Conditional verb) *to suru* or *to omou*

Adding *to suru* to the conditional or tentative form of a verb gives one of two meanings; to try to do something or to be about to do something. *Niwatori no inai aida ni tamago wo torō to shimasu.* I will try to take the egg(s) while the chicken is not there.

Typically, the second meaning of being about to do something is found in a subordinate clause followed by the final clause relating an action that prevents the subordinate clause's action from taking place. *Yasumō to shitara tonari no okusan wa shio wo kari ni kimashita.* Just as I was going to take a rest, the wife from next door came to borrow some salt.

The same conditional form of a verb followed by *to omou* says that one is considering or planning to do something. *Tokage no kunsei wo kaō to omotta ga doko mo utte imasen deshita.* I intended to buy (some) smoked lizard, but there was none on sale.

Ka mo shiremasen

Ka mo shiremasen (shirenai) can be used after nouns, pronouns, the present and past tenses of both verbs and adjectives, and even an adverb like *sō* with the sense of 'It may be...' *Kon'ya Okuyuki Fukako no kiru kimono wa midori-iro ka mo shiremasen.* The kimono that Fukako Okuyuki will wear tonight may be green.

This phrase may be used interchangeably with *ka mo wakarimasen (wakaranai).*

-shidai

-shidai attaches to the basic stem of any verb to contribute the meaning of 'as soon as.'

Tatakai ga owari-shidai itai wo atsumemashō.

As soon as the battle ends, let's gather up the bodies.

(*Tatakai* is battle, and *itai* are corpses.)

O-kyaku-san ga kaeri-shidai yasumimashō.

As soon as the guest leaves, let's go to bed.

Kikai ga ari-shidai shōkai shimasu.

As soon as there is an opportunity, I will introduce (you).

(*Kikai* is chance or opportunity.)

Sometimes the verb stem is omitted, as in:

Tōchaku shidai shachō wa kōjō ni ikimasu.

As soon as he arrives, the company president will go to
the factory. (*Tōchaku* means arrival. If *suru* is added, it
becomes a verb, to arrive.)

Cultural sidelights:

*** By now—or, soon—you should have reached the stage in your
lucubrations at which you are beginning to engage in meaningful
conversations with native speakers of Japanese. Although you will
be far from probing the theories of the dismal science of economics,
you should be well beyond the "Hello—how are you?—Well,
good-bye" stage. If so, you may be encountering the same difficulties that plagued me and my classmates in the Michigan language
school. For instance, it seemed to us that the Japanese teachers
spoke too fast and did not enunciate clearly. None could really
explain the difference between *wa* and *ga* or when to use *wa* and
when to use *wo* as accusative markers. Interpreting our English
thoughts directly into Japanese, in strict accordance with those
rules of grammar we had learned, too often elicited looks of
startled incomprehension from our teachers. This same incomprehension greeted our attempts at humor. But what I am building
up to is something else: that unsatisfactory Japanese conversations
may also be partly laid at the door of completely different styles of
conversation. American conversations are often of a confrontational
character. We seem to like excited, rapid-fire exchanges of opposing
views and sharp rebuttals. As if in a game of volley ball, we hit
the conversational ball back and forth, seeking rhetorical advan-
tage, shifting positions, even slam-dunking telling points into our
opponents' chests. We do not hesitate to raise our voices, as if
the debater with the strongest lungs deserves to win the debate. It
seems that anything short of personal contumely and angry shouting is permitted, nay, encouraged.

But such perfervid argumentation appeals not to the Japanese, with
their traditional emphasis on human harmony. They value agreement for its own sake and prefer a more sedate and orderly style
of discourse. If all are of about equal station, each participant is
usually permitted to express his opinion. When he seems to have
finished, the others wait a while to be sure he has exhausted what
he wanted to say. Seldom do they gainsay him. Usually they
murmur their agreement—or at least their acknowledgement that
they have followed his line of thought carefully. Then, in some

kind of order, the others will say whatever it is they have on their minds, while avoiding refutation, however slight or indirect, of previously expressed opinions. Interrupting another's words is the nadir of barbarism. So if—in addition to linguistic bafflements—you still are meeting embarrassed laughs or averted eyes or inexplicable silences in your verbal exchanges in Japanese, you might analyze your own style of discourse to see if it is to blame. (As an afterthought, I should add that the Japanese prefer not to become deeply involved in conversation at the dining table, where the proper activity is thought to be the consumption and enjoyment of food. An exception to this are the dinners at Japanese-style (*zashiki*) restaurants, but even there the diners tend to avoid the weightier topics. You might say that we should be able to talk and eat at the same time. Well, maybe you can, but I, for one, can't. Or if I try, I get pleasure from neither.

Kanji	On. reading(s)	Kun reading(s)	Mean-ing(s)	Stroke order	Compounds (jukugo)		
					In Kanji	Reading(s)	Meaning(s)
女	jo	onna	woman	女	女中	jochū	maid
					彼女	kanojo	she
					女の子	onnanoko	girl
八	hachi	yat(tsu)	eight	八	八日	yōka	eight days / eighth day of month
					八十	hachi-jū	eighty
中	chū	naka	middle	中	中心	chūshin	center
					夜中	yonaka	in the middle of the the night
大	tai / dai	ō(kii)	big	大	大変	taihen	very
					大切(な)	taisetsu(na)	important
					大学	daigaku	college, university
九	ku, kyū	koko-no(tsu)	nine	九	九時	kuji	nine o'clock
					九日	kokonoka	nine days / ninth day of month
小	shō	chii(sai)	small	小	小学校	shōgakkō	elementary school
					小説	shōsetsu	novel
立	ritsu	ta(tsu) / ta(teru)	to stand / to set up	立	立派(な)	rippa (na)	fine, splendid
手	shu	te	hand	手	手紙	tegami	letter
					手当	teate	treatment, allowance
子	shi	ko	child	子	子供	kodomo	child
					男の子	otokonoko	boy
					玉子	tamago	egg
母	bo	haha	mother	母	お母さん	okāsan	(your) mother

Lesson Fifteen

A.) Must
B.) Should
C.) Commands, Instructions, and Requests
D.) Permission
E.) *-ra* suffixed to the plain past.

Useful Everyday Expressions

Enryo-naku itadakimasu.	I will have some. (Lit., I will accept without reserve.) Said after your host/hostess tells you something like *Dōzo meshiagatte kudasai.*
Suki na dake nonde kudasai.	Please drink your fill.
Go-shimpai naku.	Please don't worry.
Hajimemashite.	How do you do? (Lit., For the first time.)
Motto hakkiri itte kudasai.	Please speak more clearly.
Go-shōchi no yō ni...	As you know...
O-ki wo tsukete.	Please be careful. (Kind, but not very polite.)
Asobi ni irasshatte kudasai.	Please pay (me) a visit.
Abunai yo.	Look out! (In emergencies, polite language can be dropped.)
O-jama shimasu.	Excuse me. (I'm about to bother you.)
O-jama shimashita.	I'm sorry to have intruded on you. (This is said when withdrawing.)
Dō shiyō mo nai ndesu.	It's hopeless. Nothing can be done.
O-itoma shimasu.	I have to go. I must take leave of you.
*Sō ka shira.**	I wonder if it is so.
Damare!	Shut up! (Very rough)
Kampai!	A toast! (Drain your glass!)
Komarimashita (or *Komatte imasu).*	I'm in a bind. I'm in a tough spot.**

186

Ka shira is used after most forms of speech to mean 'I wonder if...'but is said almost as if one were talking to oneself.

**If you say *Sore wa komarimashita, ne,* you are referring to someone else and mean, That's too bad, isn't it.

Komarimasu, however, is said more as a reprimand or caution against doing something. An example: *Hayaku shinai to komarimasu.* If you don't do it quickly, I will be at a loss. *Sonna mane wo shitara okāsan wa komarimasu yo.* You shouldn't act like that; it will distress your mother. (*Mane*=behavior).

Komatta is the plain past tense of *komarimashita.* Note that when *komatta* is used before a word like *hito* (person), it does not mean that the person spoken about is in distress, but that he is causing distress to someone else. Example: *Komatta shujin desu.* My husband is a distress (to me).

Vocabulary

shimeru	to shut, close	*damaru*	to keep quiet
tatoeba...	for example...	*itoma*	leave-taking
homeru	to praise	*kōshū*	public
fueru	to increase (v.i.)	*shikei*	execution, death
taishikan	embassy		penalty
tsuyoi	strong	*fukkō*	revival
kotowaru	to refuse (v.t.)	*mane*	behavior;
omoi	heavy		imitation
chawan	tea cup	*ikagawashii*	indecent,
nomu	to drink		off-color
nareru	to become	*domburi*	a china bowl in
	accustomed to		which rice and
netsu	a fever		such ingredients
hako	box		as eel, chicken,
sekai	the world		and eggs are
shūkan	custom, habit		served
doa	door	*akarui*	light, bright
dōshite	why	*ishi*	stone
umu	to bear, as a	*ie*	house
	child	*mon*	gate
umareru	to be born	*me*	eye

shumi	hobby, taste	*yakuza*	gangster
sōdan	consultation	*oyaji*	"the old man,"
tatsu	to stand		father
kōen	park	*shōchū*	low-grade distilled
shinu	to die		spirits
sekken	soap	*oikakeru*	to chase
sentaku	laundry	*urusai*	bothersome, noisy
nokoru	to remain, stay	*kissaten*	a tea-shop where
	behind		coffee and cakes
yurusu	to forgive, excuse		may also be served
tsureru	to take along, to	*kawaisō*	pitiful, pathetic,
	bring (a person)		deserving of
koibito	lover, sweetheart		sympathy
kyoka	permission		
momo-hiki *	"long johns,"		
	underpants		

*Used more by senior citizens.

Pattern Sentences

(Bunkei)

1. *Yurushite kudasai. Kesa takusan no tegami wo kakanakereba na-ranai node issho ni iku koto ga dekimasen.* Please forgive me. I have many letters to write this morning, so I cannot go with you.
2. *O-hiru made wa isogashii desu.* I am busy until noon.
3. *Saburō! Mō okiro. Hayaku gakkō ni iku nda.* Saburo! Get up (already). You should go to school quickly.
4. *Sono osoroshii hanashi wo yamete itadakitai ndesu.* I beg of you, stop the frightening stories.
5. *Kekkon no aite wa erakunakute mo yoroshii desu.* It does not matter even if your partner in marriage is not an important man.
6. *Tabako wo suwanai koto.* Do not smoke tobacco. (A written notice.)
7. *Teinei ni shite.* Do it carefully.

8. *Niwa wo kirei ni shite hoshii kara raishū ki-tamae.*
   I want you to clean up my garden so come next week.

9. *Oya no kyoka ga nakute mo Umewake Sayoko wo Roppongi no kissaten ni tsurete ikimasu.* Even without her parents' permission, I am going to take Sayoko Umewake to a Roppongi tea-shop.

10. *Yoshita hō ga ii. Sayoko no oyaji wa yakuza da kara....*
    You should stop that, because her old man is a gangster ...

11. *Kotowarimasu.* I refuse.

12. *Dō shite me ga akai ndesu ka. Mata shōchū wo nonde ita ndesu ka.*
    Why are your eyes red? Were you drinking shochu again?

13. *Ashita kara kirei na iki-jibiki wo sagashimasu.* Beginning tomorrow, I will look for a pretty 'walking dictionary.'

14. *Sā, mō yasumanakereba...* Well, I must (already) go to bed.

15. *Kodomo-tachi wa urusai kara kōsoku dōro de asobi ni tsurete itte ii yo.* Because the children are bothersome, you may take them to play on the freeway.

16. *Jimbō-san kara no tegami wo yonde kudasai-mase.* Please read the letter from Jimbo-san.

17. *Mada hayai kara taishikan no mon wo shimenakute mo ii desu.* Because it is still early, you need not close the embassy gate.

18. *Kono go-hyaku-en wo kaesanakute mo ii deshō ka.* Is it all right if I don't return this five hundred yen?

19. *Kaeshite moraimasu. Boku mo kane ga nakute komatte imasu.*
    I'll have you return it. I too am in a fix because I am flat broke.

20. *Sono poruno-zasshi wo yomu nja arimasen.* You should not read that erotic magazine.

21. *Konna omoi chawan de kōcha wo nomu to te ga tsukaremasu.*
    If I drink black tea in a heavy tea-cup like this, my hand gets tired.

22. *Naku na yo. Otoko ja nai ka!* Don't cry. You're a man, aren't you?

23. *Tatoeba, kono makka na momo-hiki de mo yoroshii desu ka.* For example, would even bright-red long johns like these be all right?

24. *Tama ni koibito wo homete kure. Kawaisō da kara...* Please praise your sweetheart now and then. Because he (she) deserves pity...

25. *Kotowatte mo kamaimasen.* It doesn't matter if you refuse.

26. *Aruitara gofun kurai desu.* If you walk, it will take about five minutes.

How to Use
Must

The meaning of 'must do' is often expressed in two words, both negative in meaning. The first word may be one of two (*nakereba* or *nakute wa*) and the second may be one of three words (*ikemasen, dame,* or *narimasen*). See chart below.

This will give us six combinations (*nakereba ikemasen, nakereba dame desu, nakereba narimasen, nakute wa ikemasen, nakute wa dame desu, nakute wa narimasen.*) Although, in a broad sense, these can be used interchangeably, there actually are some distinctions, as noted in the right-hand column below.

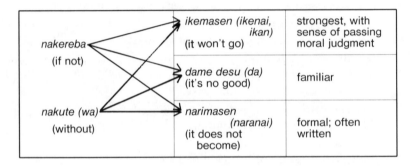

Standing alone, *nakereba* is the negative conditional form of *nai* (*arimasen*) and means, 'if there is not.' (*O-kane ga nakereba...* or, If there is no money...)

Then, as *-nakereba,* it can be attached to the negative stem of verbs (*hanasa-nakereba...* or, if you do not speak...).

This construction is not limited to use with verbs but may follow certain forms of adjectives as well. In Lesson Four, we saw that the negative of Class A adjectives is built by dropping the final *i* in the adjectives and replacing it with *ku.* To *ku* we then add *nai (arimasen), nakereba,* or *nakatta (arimasen deshita).* So the *-nakereba* under discussion can be attached to the *ku* ending of the adjective to become *akaku-nakereba...* (if it is not red...). Followed by *ikemasen, dame desu,* or *narimasen,* we have a way to say, It must be red.

If the adjective is of the B Class, we can make no changes in the body of the word itself but must follow it with *de* to realize our purpose. *Baka (na)* is the Class B adjective for foolish. If we add *de* and then one of the constructions in the chart, we will have *baka de nakereba narimasen* (or one of the other five). That is, It must be foolish.

Translated literally into English, these double-negative formulations (with the verb *inoru,* to pray, for instance) would sound awkward: If (you) don't pray, it won't go—or it's no good—or it doesn't become. Or, in the case of *nakute,* without praying, it won't go—or it's no good—or it doesn't become. (The particle *wa* may be used after *nakute* to strengthen slightly the meaning of 'without.')

Anyway, fret not. They all mean, You must do....or, It must be.

To be precise, *-nakereba narimasen* should not really be used in conversational Japanese at all except in the middle of a sentence, e.g., in a subordinate clause. However, at this stage in your studies, I advise that you not concern yourself about such niceties.

As might be expected from the Japanese penchant for incomplete sentences, the second half of the above equations can be dropped, and your meaning will still be understood. At a friend's house, if you stand and say only, *Mō ikanakereba...* (If I don't already go), he will know you mean that you must leave.

Lastly, bear in mind that the Japanese do not use their 'must' constructions quite as often as we use 'must' in English. They would never say anything like, *Anata wa dōshitemo Hamano Takako-san no unagi domburi wo tabete minakereba narimasen yo.* (You simply must try Miss Takako Hamano's eel and rice dish.) Often, when they do say 'must,' there is an underlying feeling that duty is calling. For instance, if you say at the end of an evening of carousing with a saloon crony, *Sate, uchi ni kaeranakereba ikemasen,* you thereby leave the impression that work awaits you at home and must be done that night. It would be better just to say *O-itoma shimasu.* (I will take my leave.)

Should

As we might expect, there is no exact one-word equivalent for 'should' in spoken Japanese. Instead, we must find other ways of putting across this message.

Let's work with the verb *kaku,* to write, and take its conditional form: *kakeba*—if (you) write. Thus, *Kakeba ii* (or *yoi*) becomes You *should* write. (If you write, it is good.)

If, however, you did not write and if I want to tell you that you should have, I would do it this way: *Kakeba yokatta noni...* You should have written. You see that the tense of the conditional form *kakeba* did not change, even though in English it has changed to the past. *Yokatta,* of course, is the past tense of the adjective. (We cannot make a past tense of the other reading of the same *kanji*, e.g., *ii,* there being no such word as *ikatta,*) *Noni* adds the sense of 'even though' or 'you should have' or 'I wish that.' Thus, *Kakeba*—if you write—*yokatta* (it was good)—*noni...*even. (You should have written.)

Instead of the *kakeba* above, you could say *kaitara*. As you will see below, another conditional form of the verb can be made by adding *-ra* to the plain past tense. *Kaita* being that tense of *kaku,* *kaitara* is—like *kakeba*—a conditional form: if or when (I) write. Thus,

kakeba ii	(you) should write
kaitara ii	(you) should write

Hō, as we know, means direction. Often it is used to compare two possibilities or courses of action. By saying *hō ga ii* (this direction is good) after a verb, we show that the verb's action is the better of the two courses and is something that should be done. *Kaku hō ga ii (yoi)* therewith becomes, You should write.

You can then express the meaning of 'You should not' by changing the positive form of the verb to negative *(kakanai hō ga ii)* — You should not write) or by leaving the verb in its positive form and changing the *yoi (ii)* to negative (*kaku hō ga yokunai*=the direction of writing is not good, or You should not write).

By adding *nja arimasen (nja nai)* after the dictionary form of the verb, we also express the meaning of 'should not'. *Sono tegami wo kaku nja arimasen,* means You should not write that letter.

Ndeshita or *ndatta,* after the same dictionary form of a verb means 'Should have done.' *Tegami wo kanji de kaku ndeshita.* (I) should have written the letter in *kanji.*

Let's try substituting *nja arimasen deshita* for *nja arimasen. Kodomo wo umu nja arimasen deshita.* I should not have had children. (*Umu*=to bear; *umareru*=to be born)

There are other more formal ways of expressing 'should' (such as through the use of *hazu* and *beki*), which will be addressed in the next volume of this series.

Commands, Instructions, and Requests

The several ways of asking people to do something are given in the chart below, using the verb *yomu* (to read) as an example.

Learn these constructions one at a time. Don't try to digest them all in one sitting. Practice using them and refer to the chart as necessary.

Don't use the impolite forms until you are sure of your ground. The Japanese will not want you to use them (although they themselves do), but even we *kōmō-jin* ('red-haired' foreigners) have a right to be impolite if the situation demands it.

Even so, for a while yet, your best bet is to stick with the standard polite *kudasai* after the gerund.

> *Yonde kudasai.*   Please read.

And the negative equivalent:

> *Yomanaide kudasai.*   Please do not read.

Construction of Affirmative Commands, Instructions, and Requests, Using Verb *yomu* (to read) as Example (Read; Please read)

Start with this form of verb	(Prefix, suffix, or add)	Resulting in this final form	Comment
Plain imperative *(yome)*		Yome	Very rough. Used among close male friends, in signs, quoted speech*, proverbs, military commands, urgent circumstances, sometimes by fathers to children
Basic stem *(yomi-)*	Suffix -tamae	Yomi-tamae	not polite; not used by women
Basic stem *(yomi-)*	Suffix -na	Yomi-na	This impolite usage is favored by young men who are close friends and by low-class people.
Basic stem *(yomi-)*	Prefix o; suffix na	O-yomi-na	said by low-class women
Basic stem *(yomi-)*	Prefix o	O-yomi	impolite female speech; not often used
Gerund *(yonde)*		Yonde (ne)	widely used in familiar speech, especially among women to equals, children, and subordinates
Gerund *(yonde)*	Add (o) kure	Yonde (o)-kure(yo)**	familiar speech among men
Gerund *(yonde)*	Add chōdai	Yonde chōdai(yo)	Polite; used mostly to children and subordinates
Basic stem *(yomi-)*	Suffix -nasai	(O)yomi-nasai (yo)	Used more by women than men, mostly to children, sometimes to subordinates. It may be used, however, to anyone in these fixed expressions: *o-kaerinasai, gomen-nasai, and o-yasumi-nasai.*

Affirmative Commands, Instructions, Requests *(Continued)*

Start with this form of verb	(Prefix, suffix, or add)	Resulting in this final form	Comment
Dictionary form *(yomu)*	Add *nda* (or *ndesu*)	Yomu nda; Yomu ndesu	a very direct instruction said to subordinates and children
Dictionary form *(yomu)*	Add *koto*	Yomu koto.	usually seen in signs where the authority does not have to worry about being polite.
Gerund *(yonde)*	Add *hoshii*	Yonde hoshii	"I want you to read."
Gerund *(yonde)*	Add *morau*	Yonde morau	"I'll have you read."
Gerund *(yonde)*	Add *itadakitai*	Yonde itadakitai	"I beg you to read."
Gerund *(yonde)*	Add *kudasai (-mase)*	Yonde kudasai (-mase)	"Please read." (Addition of *-mase* enhances politeness.)
Gerund *(yonde)*	Add *kudasaimasen ka.*	Yonde kudasaimasen ka.	"Won't you kindly favor me by reading?"

* 'Quoted speech' refers to those times when you are reporting what someone said to you. Suppose a man hands you a letter and says, *Kore wo yonde kudasaimasen ka.* Won't you please read this? Later, when you tell a third person about this, you would not say, *(Dare-dare)-san ga kono tegami wo yonde kudasaimasen ka to iimashita.* Mr. (So-and-so) said, Won't you please read this letter? By reporting that Mr. (So-and-so) used a polite verb like *'kudasaimasen ka'* to you—even though he actually did so, you are unduly emphasizing the respect paid you. Instead, you should say, *(Dare-dare)-san ga kono tegami wo yome to iimashita.* By using the rough imperative *yome* in place of *yonde kudasaimasen ka,* you are humbling yourself in the approved fashion. *(Dare-dare) -san* is literally Mr. (Who-who.)

** Although *yo* is generally to be thought of as a spoken exclamation mark, it is used in this case to enhance a feeling of intimacy and actually softens the directness of *Yonde kure.*

Negative Commands, Instructions, Requests: *("Don't read")*

Start with this form of verb	(Prefix, suffix, or add)	Resulting in this final form	Comment
Gerund *(yonde)*	Add *wa ikemasen*	*Yonde wa ikemasen*	Reasonably polite but not for use to superiors.
Dictionary form *(yomu)*	Add *na*	*Yomu na.*	Strong, short, certainly not polite. Use to children and servants.
Negative stem *(yoma-)*	Suffix *-nai;* add *koto*	*Yomanai koto*	Used in written notices to those within your power
Dictionary form *(yomu)*	Add *nja arimasen (nja nai)*	*Yomu nja arimasen.*	Direct instruction. Not for use to those of superior rank.
Negative stem *(yoma-)*	Suffix *-naide;* add *kudasai*	*Yomanaide kudasai*	Standard polite negative.
Negative stem *(yoma-)*	Suffix *-naide;* add *hoshii*	*Yomanaide hoshii*	"I desire your not reading" or "Don't read."

Permissions

The standard way to ask permission (in Japanese, permission =
kyoka) is to take a gerund and follow it with *mo ii desu ka,* which
gives the literal meaning, Even if **(I)** do (whatever it is), is it all
right? *Kono pūru de oyoide mo ii desu ka.* Is it all right to swim in
this pool? *Asu kōen ni itte mo ii desu ka.* Is it all right to go to the
park tomorrow?

In lieu of *ii*, you may, of course, use *yoi* or *yoroshii* or *kamaima-sen* (it doesn't matter). *Takai no wo katte mo yoroshii desu ka.* Is it all right to buy the expensive one? *Nihongo de setsumei shite mo kamaimasen ka.* May I explain it in Japanese? Lit., Even if (I) explain it in Japanese, does it not matter?

Note that in common parlance, the *mo* after the gerund is some-times omitted with no change in the meaning. *Sō omotte ii desu ka.* Is it all right if I think so? The answer could be, *Sō omotte ii desu.* It is all right to think so.

Usually, however, the person giving the permission does not repeat the entire formula, but only the final operative words. *Ii desu; Yoroshii desu; Yoi desu.* (All three mean It is all right.) Or, if *kamai-masen* (it doesn't matter) is used in the question, he or she may answer *Kamaimasen.* (Note that the affirmative form of *Kamaimasen* is not used. That is, we don't say *kamaimasu* to mean that it *does* matter.)

Instead of a gerund, the *mo ii* phrase can be used after nouns and adjectives. *Teppō wa nai ga pisutoru de mo ii desu ka.* (I) don't have a rifle, but will a pistol be all right? *Jochū wa minikukute mo yoi desu ka?* Does it matter even if the maid is ugly? (In these times of rising expectations, maids dislike being called *jochū.* They prefer 'home-helpers' or *hōmu-herupā.*)

A negative gerund is used to ask permission *not* to do something. *Kono nama-zakana wa tabenakute mo yoroshii desu ka.* May I not eat this raw fish? (Even if not eating raw fish—is it all right? *Nama-zakana* literally is raw fish, whereas the two *kanji* for *sashimi* actually mean 'stab-flesh.' There is such a thing as beef *sashimi,* too. *Sapporo biiru de nakute mo ii deshō ka.* Would it be all right even if it is not Sapporo beer?

In refusing permission, we do not usually say the negative form of *ii* or *yoi* or *yoroshii.* That is, in refusing to grant someone permis-sion to sing a hymn *(Sambika wo utatte mo yoi desu ka),* it is better not to answer *Utatte mo yoku-nai (yoku-arimasen)* or even merely *Yoku-nai.* Instead, the standard refusal is *Ikemasen* or *Dame desu.*

-ra suffixed to the plain past

In Lessons Five and Six we treated of plain past tenses and conditional (if or when) forms of Conjugation A and Conjugation B verbs.

Here we will show how to change the plain past tense of a verb to the conditional form: As an example, take the intransitive verb *tobu,* to jump (or to fly). Its plain past tense is *tonda* (I jumped); its conditional is *tobeba* (if or when I jump).

Now, if we merely suffix *-ra* to the plain past tense *(tonda),* we have another way to express the conditional.

tonda	I jumped
tobeba	if or when I jump
tondara	if or when I jump

Study recommendations

For many years foreigners have been advised that if they wish to learn Japanese quickly, they should make close friends with members of the opposite sex. It is, I can safely assert, more stimulating to discuss the many topics that lovers talk about* than to try to extol the machinery of a CAT-scanner to a hospital director from Chiba.

There is, however, a caution that I must add. While practicing Japanese with someone in front of a warm fire or over a cold martini will be most beneficial, you must take care not to let your speech patterns take on feminine traits, if you are male, or masculine characteristics, if you are female. Specific advice will be given in a subsequent volume.

The mostly neutral words and sentences herein (except where male and female distinctions are specified) will serve you well without detracting from your sexual identity, whatever it is.

*"Ah, youth's sweet-scented manuscript!"

Kanji	On Reading(s)	Kun Reading(s)	Meaning(s)	Stroke order	Compounds (jukugo)		
					In *Kanji*	Reading(s)	Meaning(s)
父	fu	chichi	father	父	お父さん	otōsan	(your) father
十	jū	tō	ten	十	十三	jū-san	thirteen
					三十	san-jū	thirty
					十日	tōka	ten days
							tenth day of month
百	hyaku		one hundred	百	五百	go-hyaku	five hundred
左	sa	hidari	left	左	左手	hidari-te	the left hand
右	u, yu	migi	right	右	右手	migi-te	the right hand
田	den	ta	rice field	田	田舎	inaka	the country
					本田	Honda	family name
止	shi	to(maru)	to stop (v.i.)	止			
		to(meru)	to stop (v.t.)				
千	sen	chi	one thousand	千	五千	go-sen	five thousand
目	moku	me	eye	目	駄目（な）	dame (na)	no good, useless
心	shin	kokoro	heart	心	心配（する）	shimpai (suru)	(to) worry
					安心する	anshin suru	to feel at ease, not worried

Lesson Sixteen

A.) The Comparative Degree
B.) The Superlative Degree
C.) The same as...
D.) *Nara*

Useful Everyday Expressions

Ōki na o-sewa da.	None of your business.
Shaku da nā!	How exasperating!
Kirei desu, nē.	(She) is pretty, isn't (she)?
Tasukarimasu.	That will be a help to me (when accepting an offer of aid).
Gambatte kudasai. (Or, among close friends, *Gambare.*)	Keep trying. Hang in there. Chin up.
Go-busata shite orimasu.	I regret not having kept in touch with you.
Shimatta!	Damn!
O-medetō (gozaimasu).	Congratulations.
Go-meiwaku deshō ga....	I'm sure this will be a bother, (but)...
Dōzo go-yukkuri...	Please make yourself at home. Please relax. (Lit., Please—honorable—slowly) Usually said when offering hospitality to a visitor in your home.
Dō iu imi desu ka. (Or, *Nan no imi desu ka.*)	What does this mean?
Daiji ni shite kudasai.	Please treat (it) with care. Please pay attention to (it). This can be used when urging consideration for anything from the conservation of rice to the training of your spouse.

Vocabulary

inoru	to pray	*saisho*	first
inori	prayer	*saigo*	last
aji	taste, flavor	*hōhō*	means, way, method
naraberu (v.t.)	to line up, to stand side by side	*haru*	spring (season)
		kutsu	shoe
hambun	half	*hayai*	fast, swift
yameru	to stop, give up (v.t.)	*sashimi*	raw fish
sampo	a walk, stroll	*nikui*	hateful, spiteful, hard
*hiku***	to pull, draw	*hidoi*	harsh (as in treatment), severe (as in storm), terrible (as in appearance)
aoi	blue (as in sky), green (as in traffic light), pale (as in face)		
tebukuro	glove	*kōtsū shingō*	traffic signal or light
umai	tasty, also skillful		
sakura no ki	cherry tree	*jinkō*	population
sakura no hana	cherry blossom	*mottomo*	most
		saishin	newest
washi	eagle	*saikō*	highest
nigeru	escape, flee	*ondo*	temperature (of air or water)
waga-kuni	our country		
suppai	sour	*taion*	temperature (of body)
au	to fit, suit	*arashi*	storm
senshi suru	to die in war	*nyūin suru*	to enter a hospital
kashikoi	intelligent, smart	*josei****	a female
kōhei (na)	fair	*kyōju*	professor
narabu (v.i.)	to stand in a line	*sagasu*	to search, look for
*totemo**	by no means, not at all, very	*shikashi*	however. This word is also used when the speaker wishes to introduce a new topic.
saku	to bloom		
jukutatsu suru	to become expert in		
		hikui	low (in stature), low (in voice)

* *Totemo* was originally used only in the negative sense, but nowadays it often means 'very' in the positive: very (pretty), very (big), very (poor), and so forth.

** *Kaze wo hiku:* to catch (or 'pull') a cold.

*** Take care with the pronunciation. Many students say this word as if the *o* were long, but it is not. *Jōsei* would mean situation, circumstances.

Pattern Sentences

(Bunkei)

1. *Ichiban wakari-yasui kotoba de setsumei shite hoshii desu.*   I want you to explain in the words that are easiest to understand.
2. *Umai fugu no sashimi nara Shimonoseki ni ryokō shita hō ga ii desu.*   If it's tasty raw blow-fish (you want), it would be better if you travelled to Shimonoseki.
3. *Sekai de jinkō no ichiban ōi kuni wa dore desu ka.*   Which country has the largest population in the world?
4. *Isogashii nara ato de kimasu.*   If you are busy, I will come later.
5. *Motto yasukute karui kutsu wa nai deshō ka.*   Don't you have any shoes that are less expensive and lighter?
6. *Waga-kuni no tame nara nan de mo shimasu.*   If it's for the sake of our country, I would do anything.
7. *Kyonen no haru ni totemo kirei na sakura no hana ga sakimashita.* Very pretty cherry blossoms bloomed in the spring of last year.
8. *Kōtsū shingō wa aoi yo. Hayaku itta hō ga ii.*   The traffic signal is green! You should go quickly.
9. *Watakushi wa washi nara kono buta-bako kara tonde nigemasu.* If I were an eagle, I would fly away from this jail (lit., pig-box).
10. *Sore yori mo ii hōhō wa arimasen ka.*   Isn't there a way that is better than that?
11. *Fumiko-san no yori Mayumi-san no ashi ga nagai yō desu.* It seems as if Fumiko's legs are longer than Mayumi's.
12. *Issen-nin to ichiman-nin to dotchi ga ōi desu ka.*   Which is more: a thousand people or ten thousand people?
13. *Kore de yokattara dōzo...* If this will do, please (take or use it.)

How to Use

The Comparative Degree

In English, we express the comparative and superlative degrees by changing the form of adjectives (sweet, sweeter, sweetest) or by using the adverbs more or most before those adjectives (more sweet, most sweet). The Japanese do not do it exactly this way.

Instead, they express the idea of 'more' by one of the three following formulations:

    a. Positioning *motto* before the adjective.

    b. As treated in the previous lesson, using *hō* (direction) followed by *ga* and then the adjective.

    c. Using this formula: subject—as for—(noun) *yori*—is (large, red, sweet, sad, or whatever). *Yori*='than'.

Saying *motto* before an adjective is the simplest method. You and your spouse may be discussing your neighbors, and you may say, *Hisaya-san wa kashikoi ndesu.* Hisaya is smart. Your spouse's rejoinder might be, *Shikashi, Osamu-san wa motto kashikoi desu.* But Osamu is smarter.

Or your spouse could have said, *Osamu-san no hō ga kashikoi desu.* Osamu is smarter. By using 'the direction of' *(no hō ga)* device, he or she has obviated the necessity of saying *motto.*

If the matter of the neighbors' intelligence has been raised in a question like, *Hisaya-san to Osamu-san to dochira no hō ga kashikoi ka shira* (I wonder which is smarter, Hisaya or Osamu?), it can be answered without resort to either device: *Osamu-san wa kashikoi no da.* (Lit., Osamu is smart, but it actually means, Osamu is smarter.)

In the previous lesson it was explained that *hō ga ii* after a verb means You should... but, of course, put another way, this can be translated in a comparative sense. That is, *Sonna ni hidoi futsukayoi nara sugu nyūin shita hō ga ii* can be rendered as either, For a hangover like that, you should immediately enter the hospital, or, For a hangover like that, (the direction of) entering the hospital is better.

The third of the methods can be illustrated like this: *Kagoshima no josei wa Tōkyō no josei yori shinsetsu desu.* The women of Kagoshima are kinder than the women of Tokyo.

Or the same thought could be expressed as, *Tōkyō no josei yori Kagoshima no josei no hō ga shinsetsu desu.* (Lit., Tokyo women—more than—Kagoshima women—direction of—kind—are.)

Yori does not need always to follow a noun, as above.

Hataraku yori asobu hō ga tanoshii desu. It is more pleasant to play than to work. (Here *yori* follows the verb *hataraku,* to work.)

Akai yori kuroi hō ga anata ni aimasu. The black suits you more than the red. Without changing the meaning, the word order may be changed to *Kuroi hō ga akai yori anata ni aimasu.*

A noun may be omitted after one adjective if it is replaced by *no.* *Akai no yori kuroi momo-hiki ga anata ni ni-aimasu.* Black long-johns suit you more than red ones. Or, *Kuroi momo-hiki ga akai no yori anata ni ni-aimasu.* (Same meaning as the previous.)

The same as...

If the two things under the comparative glass are about equal, we express this with the words *to onaji gurai. Kuroi momo-hiki wa akai no to onaji gurai ni-aimasu.* The black long johns suit you about as well as the red (...the same as the red).

Since the word *gurai (kurai)* means 'about,' we assume that the suitability of the black long-johns versus the red long-johns is not exactly the same. To introduce the idea of more exact suitability, we insert the adverb *chōdo,* for 'just.'

> *Anata ni kuroi momo-hiki wa akai momo-hiki to chōdo onaji gurai ni-aimasu.*
> On you, the black long-johns look just as good as the red ones.

The Superlative Degree

The superlative is easier to construct. You merely use one of two words (*ichiban* for 'number one' or *mottomo* for 'most') before either a Class A or Class B adjective:

A.	*mottomo ōkii*	*ichiban ōkii*	the largest
A.	*mottomo amai*	*ichiban amai*	the sweetest
A.	*mottomo suppai*	*ichiban suppai*	the sourest
B.	*mottomo kichigai*	*ichiban kichigai*	the craziest
B.	*mottomo kokkei*	*ichiban kokkei*	the funniest

Remember that the desiderative suffix *-tai* on the basic stem of a verb results in an adjectival construction which can be used with the superlative adverb *ichiban* like this: *Konya ichiban tabetai mono wa nan deshō ka.* What is it that you want most to eat tonight? *Mottomo* cannot, however, be used in place of *ichiban*. (Please don't ask me why; I don't know.)

Mottomo is written with a *kanji* whose *on* reading is *sai,* and which is often found in compound *kanji* to import the sense of 'most.' For instance, the two *kanji* whose *kun* readings would be *mottomo* and *atarashii* (new) can be combined to make *saishin,* meaning the newest. Or those for *mottomo* and *takai* come together as *saikō* or the highest. Then *saikō* may be joined with another compound like *ondo* ('warmth' and 'degree') to make *saikō ondo* or the highest temperature. Often these are written forms, but *saikō ni* may be used idiomatically, as in, *Kyō wa saikō ni atsui ndesu.* (Today is the hottest.)

Nara follows the present or past tenses of verbs, nouns, pronouns, and adjectives, with the meaning of 'if.'

Oishii nara	If it is delicious
Arashi ga kuru nara	If a storm is coming
Kichigai nara	If crazy

Anata nara	If (it is) you
Okusan ga nigeta nara	If your wife has run off
Senshi shita nara	If (he) died in battle

Nara may also be used after an honorific verb stem, which is the basic stem of a verb with the prefix *o:*

> *Shachō ga o-tsukai nara kashite agemasu.*
> I will lend (it) if the president is going to use it.

Naraba and *nara* mean the same and are interchangeable, but the former is more literary in tone.

Study recommendations

When we students entered the Japanese language school at the University of Michigan in 1943, we were given several language textbooks. Of these, the one we used most (probably because it was written by the head of the school) was *Modern Conversational Japanese* by Dr. Joseph K. Yamagiwa. (My edition was published in 1942 by McGraw-Hill, but it would surprise me if you could find a copy on sale anywhere, unless in a rare old book store.)

Anyway, as my final study recommendation in this volume, I want to quote one sentence from Dr. Yamagiwa's preface, which is as valid today as it was then:

"…when all is said and done, the best way to learn (Japanese) is to speak it, daringly, on the basis of acceptable examples."

When we asked Dr. Yamagiwa exactly what he meant by "acceptable examples," he replied, "the pattern sentences in your textbooks."

So engrave the pattern sentences on your livers and speak forth daringly.

Cultural sidelights:

***   If you have studied assiduously, you may find—as you come to
the end of this first volume—that more and more frequently you
are receiving glowing tributes from the Japanese on your ability
in their language.

The easiest way to respond to these congratulations is to say merely,
Dō itashimashite. (Don't mention it. It's really not worthy of your
notice.)

If you feel that this disclaimer is inadequate, you might try one
of these:

Mada shoho no dankai desu.
I'm still at the beginner's stage.
Taishita koto wa arimasen.
It's nothing to brag about.
Mina-sama no o-kage de sukoshi dekiru yō ni narimashita.
Thanks to everyone's help, I can speak a little.
Mada heta desu ga isshōkemmei ni yatte imasu.
I'm still poor at it, but I'm trying my best.
Motto hayaku jōzu ni nareba ii noni...
If only I could improve more quickly...

The danger, however, is that you may allow their often lavish
commendations to influence your self-evaluation. Beguiled, you
may then relax your efforts or, worse, abandon your studies
altogether—to spend your time basking in the admiration of
Japanese friends.

Even though they often utter their eulogies in an almost formulaic
manner, understandably your heart will warm to their gracious
words, but don't let their homage lull you into complacency. You
have made a good start but still have a long row to hoe. Their
hurrahs will follow you along that row, but you will find there is
little difference between the acclaim they give you when you know,
say, 50 words and that which they will give you when your
vocabulary has grown to 10,000 words.

Indeed, you may then appreciate the significance of the proverb,
"Praise of the unworthy is robbery of the deserving."

So push ahead. Don't falter. You will find that the more you learn,
the faster you learn. You will meet two shadowy fiends on the
road ahead—Frustration and Discouragement—but if you have
come this far, you must have what it takes to go the rest of the way.

Kanji	On Reading(s)	Kun Reading(s)	Meaning(s)	Stroke order	Compounds (jukugo) In Kanji	Reading(s)	Meaning(s)
万	man		ten thousand	万	一万	ichi-man	ten thousand
口	kō	kuchi	mouth	口	人口	jinkō	population
見	ken	miru	to see, look	見	意見	iken	opinion
入	nyū	hai(ru)	to enter	入	入口	iriguchi	entrance
		i(reru)	to put into				
行	kō, gyō	iku	to go	行	旅行	ryokō	travel, trip
					銀行	ginkō	a bank
男	dan	otoko	man	男	男女	danjo	men and women
					長男	chōnan	eldest son
					男の子	otoko no ko	boy
書	sho	kaku	to write	書	書き言葉	kaki-kotoba	written language
					書店	shoten	book store
年	nen	toshi	year	年	今年	kotoshi	this year
					来年	rainen	next year
					去年	kyonen	last year
足	soku	ashi	foot	足	足音	ashioto	sound of foot steps
					足代	ashidai	traveling expenses
外	gai	soto	outside	外	外国	gaikoku	foreign country
					以外(の)	igai (no)	unexpected
		hoka	other		外相	gaisō	the Foreign Minister